THE COMPLETE BOOK OF
Children's
ACTIVITIES

KINGFISHER BOOKS
Grisewood & Dempsey Inc.
95 Madison Avenue
New York, New York 10016

First American edition 1993
2 4 6 8 10 9 7 5 3 1

Library of Congress Cataloging-in-Publication Data
Rice, Melanie.
The complete book of children's activities / Melanie Rice. — 1st American ed.
p. cm.
1. Creative activities and seatwork—Juvenile literature.
2. Amusements—Juvenile literature. 3. Educational games—Juvenile
literature. I. Title.
LB1140.35.C74R53 1993
372.13′078—dc20 92–30859 CIP

ISBN 1-85697-907-5

Printed in Spain
Editor: Jacqui Bailey
Assistant Editor: Deri Robins
Design: The Pinpoint Design Company
Photography: Rex Caves
Cover Design: The Pinpoint Design Company

Acknowledgments
The author would like to thank her husband, Chris, for all his
invaluable advice and support during the preparation of this book.

For permission to include copyright material, acknowledgment and
thanks are due to the following:
Daphne Lister for "In the Rain" from *Gingerbread Pigs and Other Rhymes*, © 1980.
Little, Brown and Company for "Eletelephony" from *Tirra Lirra; Rhymes Old and New*
by Laura Richards, copyright 1930, 1932 by Laura E. Richards; © renewed 1960 by
Hamilton Richards. Spike Milligan and Spike Milligan Productions Ltd. for "Rain" and
"Bump" from *Silly Verse for Kids*. A.A. Milne and Methuen Children's Books for "Lines
and Squares" from *When We Were Very Young*. Marian Reiner on behalf of Lilian
Moore "Go Wind Go" from *I Feel the Same Way* © copyright 1967 by Lilian Moore.
Ogden Nash and Curtis Brown Ltd. for "Hands" from *Family Reunion*, © Ogden
Nash. Reproduced on behalf of the estate of Ogden Nash by Curtis Brown Ltd.,
London. Clive Sansom and A. & C. Black Publishers Ltd. for "The Airman" and "I Wish
I Could" from *Speech Rhymes*. Ruth Sansom and A. & C. Black Publishers Ltd. for
"Elephant Walk" and "Going to the Sea" from *Rhythm Rhymes*. Ian Serraillier for
"The Tickle Rhymes" from *The Monster Horse*. While every effort has been made to
obtain permission, there may still be cases in which we have failed to trace a copyright
holder. The publisher will be happy to correct any omission in any future reprint.

THE COMPLETE BOOK OF
Children's
ACTIVITIES

Melanie Rice

illustrated by

Chris Barker

adviser

Betty Root

Kingfisher Books

NEW YORK

Introduction

The Complete Book of Children's Activities is a compilation of ideas drawn from my experience of bringing up two young children. It was then that I discovered first hand just how long the hours can seem between breakfast and bedtime! With household chores and demanding minds competing for my attention all day, I usually found that despite good intentions, very little of my time was spent actually playing with the children. I hope that this book will provide parents who also have "good intentions" with a source of reference; inspiring them to make the most of the rewarding hours spent in the company of their preschool children.

Parent and Child Together
Parents learn a great deal about their children by observing them while they play and by listening to them recalling their experiences. Listening is particularly important; while it is easy to talk to children, listening requires more patience—it's all too tempting to interrupt or finish sentences which seem to falter or stray from the point.

Children learn from their parents through conversation as well as through other stimuli—poems, pictures, games, and so on. And because of the special intimacy that exists between parent and child, each activity can be directly related to the world they share.

But do remember that the emphasis in this book is on the word "play." Children learn much more quickly and easily when they are absorbed and interested in what they are doing. Never force your children into an activity; if they begin to get bored, do something else. Children are also quick to pick up on the moods of their parents, so if you are bored, that is another good reason to do something else.

Using This Book
In making the selection of activities, I have tried to include only those that are readily accessible, which generally need little preparation and use materials close to hand, and which do not require special outings to provide stimulation.

The activities have not been arranged according to age; this type of categorization seemed irrelevant to me, as every child has a different rate of development. No doubt you too have been irritated by being told that a "three-year-old should be able to ..." when it's clear that, whatever the activity, children proceed at their own pace. While no amount of pushing can force them to begin learning before they're ready, once they've started it is impossible to stop them.

What Will They Learn?
The ideas in this book have been designed to help children acquire a variety of skills, enabling them to explore and interpret their world.
Manual dexterity: The practiced use of tools, such as paintbrushes, pencils, and scissors, develops coordination and helps prepare children for the difficult skill of writing.
Language: Planning activities together, carrying them out, and talking about them afterwards, improves vocabulary, stimulates conversation, and develops understanding.

Listening: Children need practice in listening skills, whether for pleasure (listening to interesting sounds, stories, or music) or for information (following simple instructions). Powers of concentration are also enhanced.

Imagination: Creativity is stimulated by giving children the freedom to explore colors, shapes, and textures.

Observation: The ability to distinguish basic patterns and shapes (which is all written words mean to children) is a skill they need to acquire before they begin reading. Looking closely at the details in pictures helps to develop this skill.

Reading: Children learn to read only when they are ready, but you can encourage their interest in books in several ways: by reading yourself, by reading to your children, and by looking at books with them (well-illustrated adult reference books as well as children's picture books).

Writing and numbers: Drawing the child's attention to words and numbers all around him or her—on buses, houses, store signs, food packages etc.—will help in appreciating the importance of the written word and in understanding it.

A Few Tips

Before starting a play session, bear the following in mind:

1. Atmosphere—a happy relaxed atmosphere is essential if a child is going to benefit from the play session.

2. Timing—a tired or hungry child will be inattentive; and interruptions spoil concentration.

3. Location—some activities need plenty of room, others are messy, and mopping up equipment needs to be on hand.

During a session:

1. Encouragement—constant praise, even for the smallest achievement, will help develop a child's confidence and ability to learn new things.

2. Striking a balance—it's not easy to sit back and watch children explore and discover without succumbing to the temptation of imposing your own ideas in order to speed up the process. Yet only by probing for themselves can children come to a real understanding of the world. Try to work alongside the child rather than leading.

3. Pace—introduce new ideas slowly and carefully and give plenty of practice with new skills.

4. Success—don't dwell on things that seem difficult. Instead, find something your child is comfortable with and can be positive about.

And afterward:

Sharing—display the best work for friends and other members of the family to see and admire.

Finally, remember that for both of you, the main thing is that the whole exercise should be tremendous fun!

Contents

Matching and numbers 65

Wordplay 93

Making Things

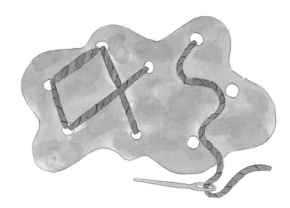

Gathering materials

Here are some ideas for building up your "art box," but no doubt you will have plenty of others of your own.

As a general rule, introduce things to your child gradually—too much to choose from at any one time can be overwhelming. Occasionally put things away for a few months to prevent boredom.

To begin with, look around the house—even trash may turn out to be useful—so start collecting:

Containers
Lids from jars or aerosol cans, yogurt, margarine or cottage cheese containers, styrofoam meat trays, aluminum foil trays and other prepacked food cartons, egg cartons, matchboxes, cupcake cases, cans—such as cocoa or bandaid cans, with firm lids—and plastic bottles.

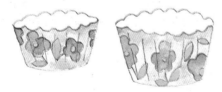

Paper
Newspaper, magazines, catalogs, old Christmas and birthday cards, postcards, tissue paper, foil, paper doilies, gift paper, computer printout paper, wallpaper, and straws.

Cardboard
Backs of notepads, corrugated cardboard, tubes from rolls of paper towels or toilet tissue, shirt cards, cereal boxes.

Scraps of Material
Any kind, but especially fur, tweed, lace, burlap, velvet, corduroy, old shirts or sheets, rug scraps, feathers, fringing, ribbons, sponge, yarn.

Odds and Ends
String, shoelaces, rubber bands, pipe cleaners, buttons, beads, curtain rings, sequins, seeds, nuts, cereal, macaroni, empty spools, toothpicks, woodshavings, corks, aluminum foil, and plastic bottle tops.

Paint
1 Large plastic bottles of poster paint. Only put out a little to use at a time.

2 Powder paint. This is cheaper but messier. Mix it yourself to the consistency of heavy cream. If it dries out, add a few drops of hot water and leave for a couple of hours.

3 Watercolor paints. These come in boxes and are economical and clean to use. But they aren't good for experimentation with textures and are ineffective on colored paper.

Painting Tips
When mixing paint it tends to go further if you add a little wallpaper paste to it.

If you add a little detergent to paint it makes it easier to remove from clothes.

If you run out of paint, use flour mixed with water and food coloring.

Palettes for Holding Paint

Use yogurt containers (or the tops of aerosol cans) placed on a tray. Or use an old cupcake tray with separate compartments.

> *Warning:* When children first paint they splash their brush enthusiastically from one color to the other until the paints become muddy. Don't interfere—they will soon realize that it's better to keep the colors separate.

Paste

1. Wallpaper paste. Cheap and useful for sticking paper together and for thickening paint.
2. Flour and water. Mix to a thick consistency.
3. Water-soluble adhesive. There are a number of non-toxic, all-purpose adhesives on the market made for use by children.

Brushes

1. Buy large sizes to encourage bold brush strokes.
2. Sometimes use 1 inch hardware brushes—they can often be better than art brushes.
3. Keep a separate brush for paste, or use a piece of cardboard.

Wash all brushes in soapy water when finished, and store them flat in newspaper to keep their shape.

Crayons and Chalks

Buy extra-thick wax crayons and the thickest types of chalk and charcoal (they don't break so easily). Peel off any paper so that the sides can be used as well.

Clay or Dough

1. Clay of a type which hardens without being baked is available, but it is very expensive.
2. Modeling clay is softer and easier to manipulate. You can make your own play dough. At first, use the recipe that is given here, but later try experimenting with the amounts. It will keep indefinitely in an airtight plastic bag or tub.

Dough Recipe
2 cups flour
2 tbs cooking oil
1 cup water
1 cup salt
Add paint or food coloring as wanted.

Be Prepared

Before you start any kind of art activity, spread a large piece of plastic sheeting across the floor. It can be bought inexpensively from hardware stores and is well worth the money. Have a large bowl of soapy water, a sponge, and a mop handy!

Painting

Think of different ways to apply the paint. Spatter and splash it on. Use your fingers (most children do naturally when they begin painting), or any of the following: a comb, a brush, a piece of cardboard, a sponge, a toothbrush, string. Try putting some paint into the corner of a plastic bag. Cut a small hole in the bag and let the paint dribble onto the paper.

Experiment with interesting textures. Add soap powder, dishwashing liquid, flour, sugar, sand, adhesive, or wallpaper paste to the paint and see what happens.

Vary the surface you paint on. Try foil, corrugated cardboard, tissue paper, old magazines or newspaper, wet paper, paper brushed with cooking oil, or even cellophane—the finished product can then be hung on the window.

How to Teach Painting

The answer is, don't. It impedes natural creativity. The best you can do is to provide the materials and opportunities to stimulate the imagination and then take a back seat. Avoid asking questions like "What is it?", or "Tell me about it," when you are presented with a piece of paper apparently filled with meaningless splotches. When children paint they are expressing their feelings rather than representing particular objects; it is the act of painting that is important, rather than the finished product.

Blobbing Paint

Drop a few blobs of very thin paint onto a piece of paper and tilt it to form rivulets. As an alternative, blow paint over the paper with a straw.

Bubbles

When you have a container of thin paint, mix some dishwashing liquid into it and blow air into the pot through a small straw to make colored bubbles on the surface. When you have a fairly frothy surface, gently lay a piece of paper over the top.

Stencils

A piece of sponge is ideal for applying paint to stencils.

1 Cut a random shape from the middle of a piece of cardboard. Lay it on a piece of paper and use it as a stencil by filling the hole with paint. Or, put the shape on the paper and paint around its edge.

Try folding the paper in half and smoothing your hand firmly over the top. When the paper is open, both sides will be identical.

2 For more intricate stencils use paper doilies. You can make your own by folding a circle of paper into quarters (as shown below) and cutting out a few simple shapes.

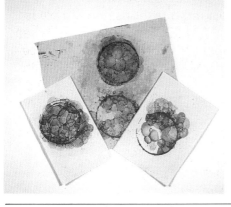

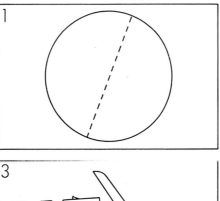

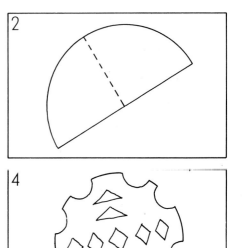

Magic painting

1 Place a thin piece of paper over any objects which have an interesting surface texture. Then rub firmly across the paper with the sides of a crayon until the pattern of the object appears.

3 Make a drawing with wax crayon, pressing heavily on the crayon. Wash over the paper with thin paint—the drawing will shine through.

For extra magic, follow the same procedure but this time use a white candle to make the drawing. The drawing will not show until the paint is applied.

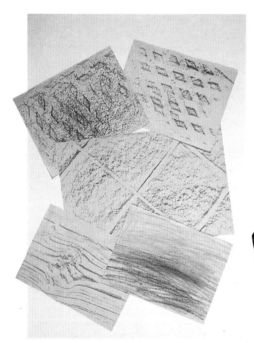

2 With a drop of glue to stop them from slipping, stick some large magazine pictures onto a piece of cardboard and cover with a sheet of white tissue paper. Paint water over the tissue, using a large brush, and watch the pictures appear.

4 Cover a sheet of heavy paper or white cardboard with brightly-colored patches of wax crayon. Now completely cover the whole paper with black crayon. Scratch away the black to form patterns. You will need to use something with a fairly sharp point, such as a knitting needle.

Finger painting

Mix flour and powder paint with water to make a thick paint. Spread onto a sheet of firm paper, a smooth tray, or a baking sheet, and let your child draw patterns in the paint with their fingers.

Color Mixing

For older children. Put out two or three colors. Let your child decide which colors to use where. Talk about the different color combinations he or she has made.

Making prints

First, you will need to make a paint pad. Mix some thick paint and add a pinch of wallpaper paste and a little detergent. Lay a piece of sponge or foam, or an old washcloth in a tray (use a styrofoam meat tray or an old baking tray) and pour the paint over the sponge.

All kinds of objects will make prints. Press them firmly onto the paint pad and then onto the paper.

String Prints

1. Dip a piece of yarn or string into the paint. Lay it on the paper with one end hanging over the edge. Fold the paper in half and, with one hand laid gently on top, slide out the piece of string.

2. Cover a cardboard tube with glue and wind a piece of string around the outside of the tube. When the glue is dry, roll the tube across the paint pad and then across a sheet of paper.

3. Dab adhesive onto a piece of paper. Drop a few odd lengths of string onto the glued paper so that they fall into curled patterns. When the glue is dry, apply thick paint to the string. Make a print of the string pattern by placing another sheet of paper on top of the string and pressing down firmly with a rolling pin.

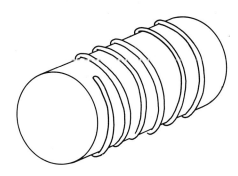

Hand and Footprints

Press feet and hands first onto the paint pad and then onto a large sheet of paper. Use fingerprints too, to make up a pattern.

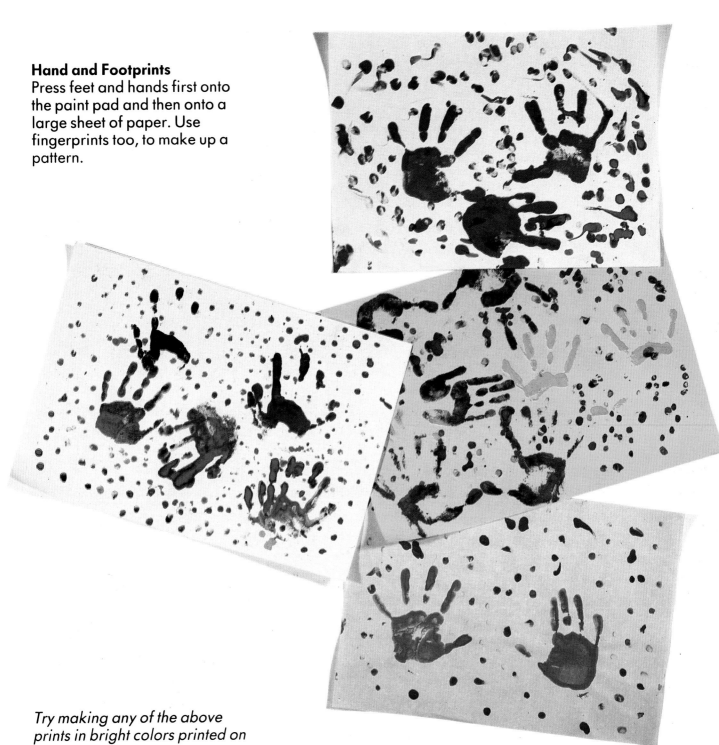

Try making any of the above prints in bright colors printed on newspaper.

Printing from Plastic

Spread a thick layer of paint mixed with adhesive onto a sheet of plastic. Scrape away patterns in the paint with a piece of cardboard. Make a print by placing a sheet of paper over the plastic.

You can clean the plastic with dishwashing liquid, but as you do, make a print of the bubbles and swirls that form when you add the detergent.

Oil on Water Prints

Half-fill a baking tray with water. Add some oil paints of different colors, or leftover household paint (but keep a solvent handy). Stir the water gently with a stick, and float a sheet of paper on the surface for half a minute. Then lift the paper at one corner and peel it off the water. Lay the paper flat to dry.

> **Warning:** This is very messy and is best done only with adult supervision.

Collage

For young children, simply spread adhesive over a piece of paper and place objects onto the surface.

Use buttons, yarn, fabrics, pipe cleaners, feathers, bottle tops, seeds, dried peas, leaves, eggshells, etc.

Use different materials as a base: cardboard, wood, or even a slab of dough.

Older children can apply glue directly to the objects. Paint some objects before gluing them, or alternatively, paint over and around them onto the paper when the glue has dried.

String Collage

String, dipped into a thick mixture of paint and paste, will stick firmly as it dries.

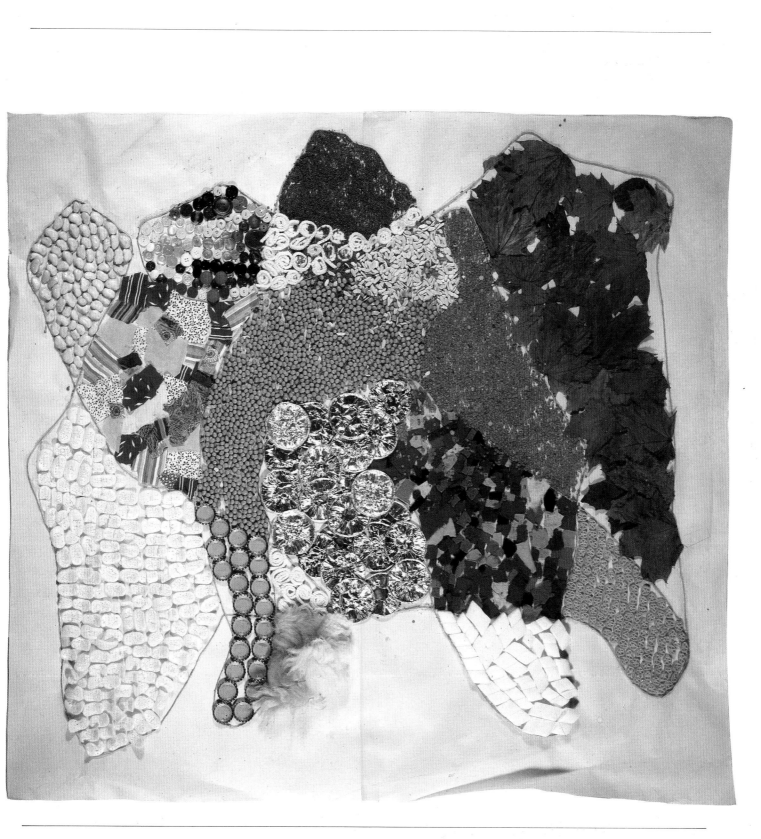

Paper collage

A wide variety of shapes and textures can be obtained just from paper. Remember that it can be torn, cut, rolled, twisted, bent, folded, crumpled, fringed, pleated, and curled.

Pleating
Lightly mark off a piece of paper into equal divisions. Fold along the marks.

Fringing
Alternatively, cut the paper three-fourths of the way along each division.

Spirals
Cut paper into a rough circle and draw a spiral as shown. Cut along the lines and hang it vertically from the center. Or, fasten at both ends so that it winds horizontally across the collage like a snake.

Curling

Wind a narrow strip of paper (not more than about 1 inch wide) around a pencil. Slide the pencil out and the paper will remain curled.

A loose curl can be made by simply pulling the paper firmly through the thumb and forefinger a few times.

Tubing

Either cut the insides of tubes of paper towels or toilet tissue into various lengths, or make your own paper tubes. These can be glued to the collage either end up or on their sides.

Drinking straws can be glued together into a pile, like logs, and then painted. (Use paint thickened with wallpaper paste.)

Paper patterns

Collect an assortment of paper, such as tissue paper, typing paper, aluminum foil, scrap paper, colored paper, cardboard, cellophane, and printed paper (newspapers, magazines, old letters, wrapping paper).

1 Make patterns using paper cut into one particular shape, such as all stars, or all circles.

2 Buy some clear plastic film which has a sticky "peel-off" backing (you can get this from most art shops or good stationery stores). Tear up some pieces of tissue paper and apply them to the sticky side of the plastic. New colors can be made by overlapping tissue of different colors. The final result can then be hung against a window so the light will shine through.

3 Cut silhouette shapes from black paper and stick them onto a colored background. Or, you could color in the background first with a finger painting.

Models

A young child can produce exciting sculptures and models using items from your art box; it does not matter at all if the early attempts are not recognizable.

Try making trains, cars, boats, people, monsters, etc. Allow your child's imagination to run wild—and before long, better models will appear than I could ever suggest.

Use cardboard boxes (for bases), tubes (for bodies or smokestacks), spools and egg cartons (heads or wheels), yogurt containers (hats), pipe cleaners, string or drinking straws (arms and legs), plastic bottles (heads or bodies), and strips cut from plastic milk cartons (arms or tentacles).

Toys and sculptures

Newspaper Trees
Roll up a sheet of newspaper and tape it lightly at one end to hold the roll in place. At the other end, use a pair of scissors to cut the roll into strips (from the center out). Cut the strips about two-thirds down the length of the roll. Pull up the inside "leaves," turning them slightly as you pull. The outside "leaves" will spread out into the shape of a tree.

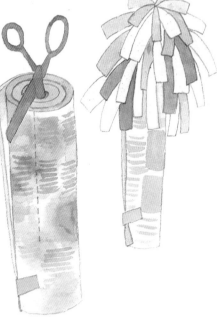

Whizzer Wheel
Cut out a circle of cardboard (with a diameter of about 5 inches) and paint colored shapes on it. Poke two holes in the center and thread a piece of yarn through them. Tie the yarn so that the wheel is in the middle of two loops. Put each hand through a loop, and twist the yarn as much as you can, holding one hand still while turning the other. Pull sharply so that the wheel spins around, then let it slacken. Continue jerking the yarn and the wheel will spin.

Spinning Top
Cut out a circle of cardboard and paint a pattern on it. An older child might try painting a spiral—you could draw the edges in first in pencil. Put a toothpick or pencil through the *center* of the card and spin it.

Windmill
Paint or print bright patterns on both sides of a piece of thin cardboard, about 6 inches square. Cut the paper from each corner to within about 1 inch of the center, as shown.

Without creasing the paper, pull the left side of each corner into the center. Thread a piece of wire through all the layers of card at the center, and twist the wire around a bead to secure the front.

Finally, thread a second bead onto the back and attach the wire firmly to the end of a stick.

Creeping Spools

Paint an empty spool and put a thick rubber band through the hole. Place a short pencil inside each end of the band. Wind up one side, put the spool on the table and watch it creep along.

Hole Sculptures

You will need some modeling clay to make a base, some tubes, and pieces of paper and cardboard with holes cut in them.

Make some holes in the clay base with a pencil—make some of the holes go straight through the base. Push the cards, tubes and paper into the clay around the holes.

As an alternative, build up a sculpture using straws, candy wrappers, cellophane, and other see-through materials.

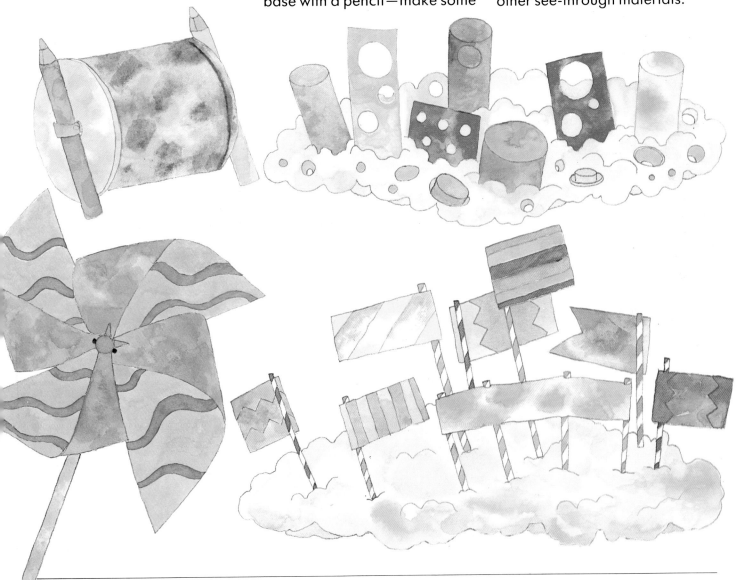

Mobiles

Mobiles are fun to make, and they are also a pleasure to look at. An older child can be encouraged to make one for any babies in the family.

Cut out some shapes from cardboard or colored paper. (Use colored foil wrapping paper. Glue the paper onto the cardboard so that it catches the sunlight; decorate the cardboard with bright colors or create a collage.)

Thread the shapes and hang them from threaded triangles of drinking straws, or two coat hangers tied together. To balance properly, the shapes need to be tied to both ends and/or to the center of the hangers.

Papier-mâché

Half-fill a large bowl with wallpaper paste and cut up small strips of newspaper. Smear the object you want to make a model from with petroleum jelly. Dip the strips of newspaper, one at a time, into the paste and place over the model until it is covered with several layers of paper. Leave to dry.

A Paper Plate
Grease the top of an old china plate with petroleum jelly. Cover the top of the plate with papier-mâché strips. When dry, trim the edges with a pair of scissors and remove the china plate from underneath.

A Mask
Grease half an inflated balloon and cover that half with papier-mâché. Allow to dry, then burst the balloon and remove it.

Trim the edges of the mask. Cut out the eye holes and paint on the decorations. You could also glue on some yarn or bits of fur for hair. Make two small holes on either side of the mask and thread through some elastic to tie the mask in place.

Paper Animals
Completely grease an inflated balloon and cover it with papier-mâché. When dry, glue on cardboard legs, ears, and tail, and paint it.

29

A playhouse

Use a large cardboard box from an appliance store (such as a refrigerator or washing-machine box). You can either leave the box whole, and simply cut a door in one side and a window in another. Or, cut off the top and bottom and open out the four sides. Cut two windows in the sides and stand it upright in the corner of a room. Prop one end against the wall, or tape it to the wall, if possible, but leave the other end open to act as a doorway. You could drape an old sheet over the top as a roof. Use smaller boxes for furniture.

An obstacle course

You can make this for dolls or, if
you have the space, for children.
 For dolls, use cardboard
boxes, matchboxes, and scraps
of material. For children use
chairs, stools, scatter cushions,
cardboard boxes, old sheets or
rugs, and pieces of newspaper.

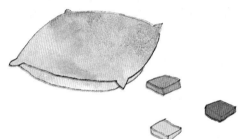

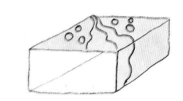

A dollhouse

Cut off the tops of four cardboard boxes and glue them together to make the four rooms of a "house." (Cardboard wine boxes tend to be a standard size, so try your local liquor store.) Add a touch of realism by cutting out windows and doorways to connect one room with another.

Decorate the boxes with scraps of wallpaper or pieces from a discarded wallpaper sample book. Furnish the rooms with objects from your art box. Some ideas are shown in the illustrations below and on the opposite page.

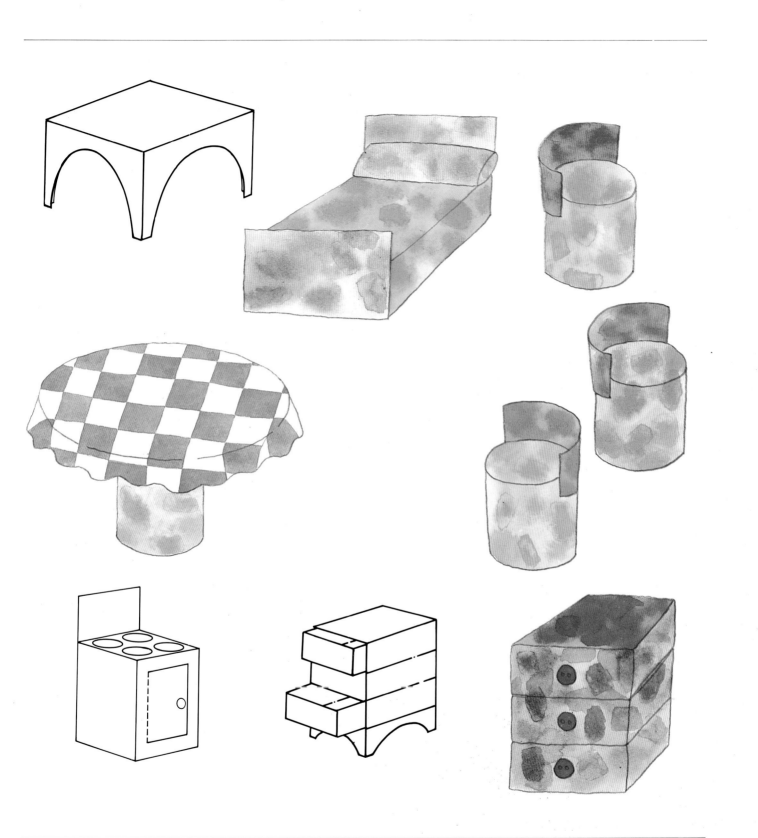

Threading and tying

Shoe Lacing
Draw a large shoe onto a piece of cardboard, or trace over the outline of the drawing shown here. Punch holes in the top of the boot and practice threading and tying shoelaces, as with an ordinary shoe.

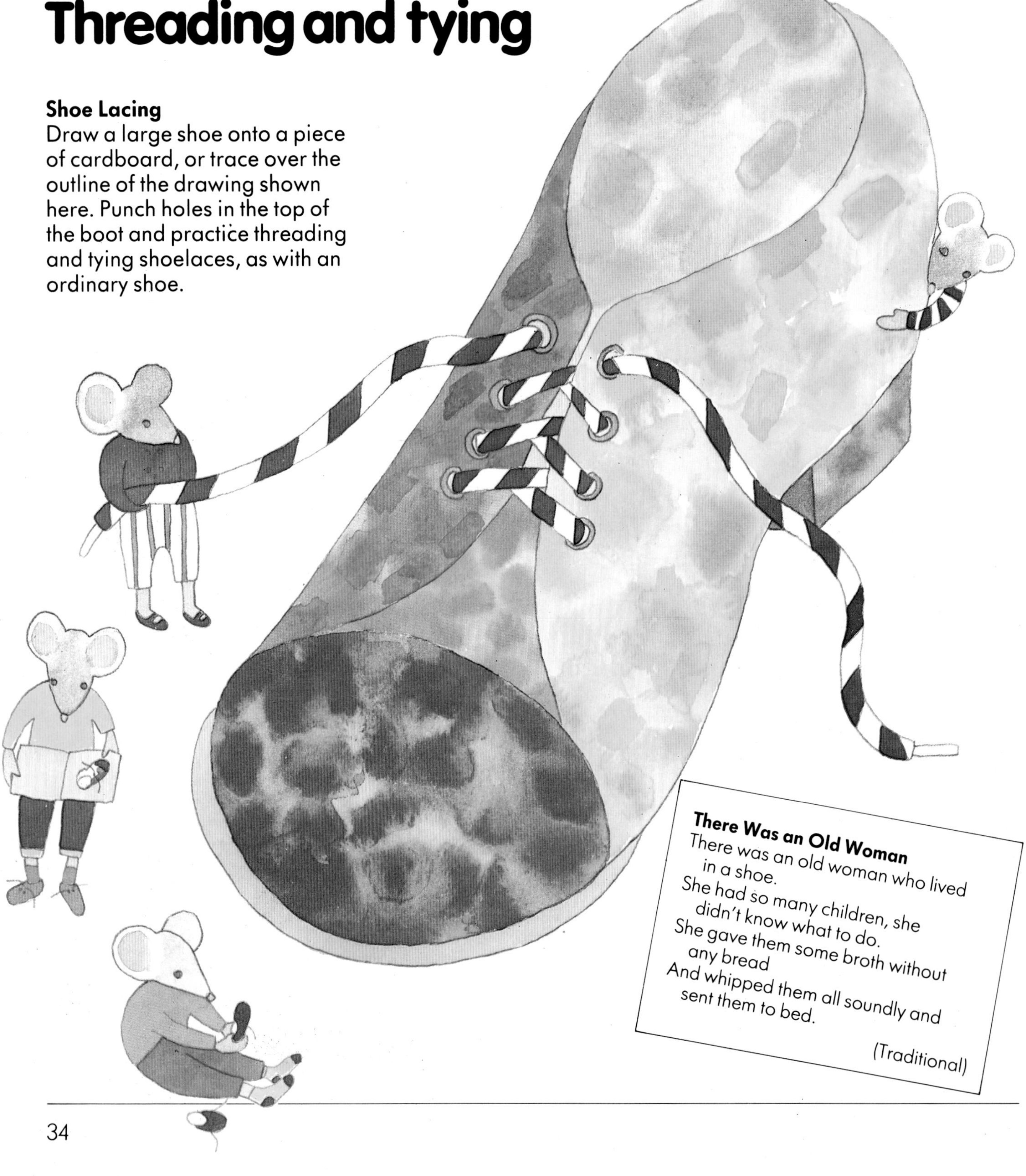

There Was an Old Woman
There was an old woman who lived in a shoe.
She had so many children, she didn't know what to do.
She gave them some broth without any bread
And whipped them all soundly and sent them to bed.

(Traditional)

Threading

1 Cut out a simple shape from a firm piece of cardboard, then cut or punch holes large enough for shoelaces to be threaded through to make a pattern.

2 Trace the shape of your child's name onto a card with punched holes. Thread through the holes with colored shoelaces.

3 Glue a picture with a clear outline onto a piece of cardboard. Punch large holes all around the edge of the picture (about 1/4 inch apart). Help your child to stitch around the picture with a large blunt needle and yarn.

4 Take some spools, or yogurt containers with holes cut in the bottom, and thread them onto string to make a snake. (Make knots in the string to keep the containers apart.)

Older children can thread macaroni (or other types of hollow pasta), pieces of colored straws, and beads onto long shoelaces.

Pompoms

Cut out two circles of cardboard the same size, and make a medium-sized hole in the middle of each. Put the two rings together and wind a ball of yarn through the middle and around the rings.

When the layers of yarn nearly fill the center hole, cut them by sliding the scissors between the two pieces of cardboard. When you have cut the yarn all the way around, pull the pieces of cardboard a little way apart and tie a strong piece of yarn firmly around the middle. Then remove the rings.

A Woolly Chicken

Make a pompom as above. Fold a pipe cleaner in half and hook it through the yarn, before you tie it in the middle and remove the rings. Use a long piece of yarn to tie the middle and leave the two ends dangling for the moment.

Make a smaller ball, and tie the middle of this ball with the same piece of yarn that you used to tie the larger one. Shape the pipe cleaners into legs, and stick a felt or cardboard beak onto the head.

36

Exploring All Around

Around the house

Explain how the electricity meter works—switch on one or two appliances and watch the dial react. Take this opportunity to warn your child of the dangers of electricity; explain about not touching loose wires, or sockets, and not playing with appliances.

Trace the route the water takes through your house by following the pipes.

Demonstrate how the radiators work. Hold some strips of paper above a radiator and watch them flutter as the warm air blows them up. Where is the air hotter—above or below the heater?

Use the telephone—listen to the different tones.

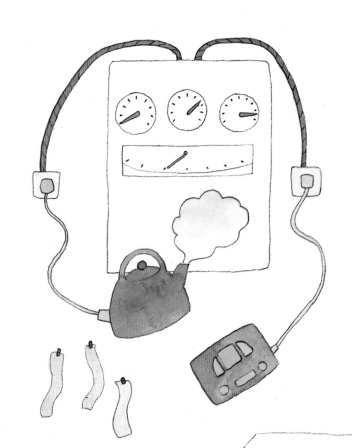

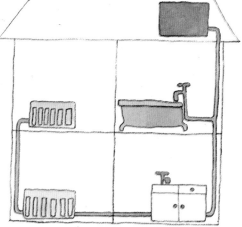

Cooking

Explain to your child about always washing his or her hands before touching food.

Give your child practice in all the various cooking tasks—measuring, counting, chopping (use a dull knife), coring, peeling, grating, mixing, stirring, rolling, etc.

Begin by letting your child help you with part of the recipe. Then, as his interest and powers of concentration grow he can gradually learn to prepare a complete dish. Older children can be shown how to use electrical appliances.

Beginners' recipes

Choose things that are quick, yet fun to make.

1 Sandwiches: Experiment with different fillings to learn which flavors go well together. This may lead to some enjoyable picnics.

Try: Tuna, cucumber, tomatoes, hard-boiled egg (sliced or mashed with mayonnaise), cheese, pickles, salami, cottage cheese, grated carrot, liverwurst, chopped celery or apple, peanut butter, honey, pineapple, banana.

2 Scrambled eggs: Melt a pat of butter in a frying pan. Beat together one egg and one tablespoon of milk and pour into the pan.

Cook gently, stirring continuously until the egg mixture sets.

As a variation, try adding one tablespoon of grated cheese just before the egg sets.

3 Fillings for crepes, pizzas, baked potatoes, and omelets: Use mushrooms, onions, cucumber, tomato, cooked or grated vegetables, cheese, egg (scrambled or hard-boiled), shrimp, chicken, ham, parsley, etc.

Cookie Recipe

1 cup all-purpose flour
1/2 cup sugar
1/4 cup butter
1 tsp baking powder
1/2 tsp vanilla extract
1/2 tsp milk
1 egg, well beaten
Pinch of salt

1. Cream the butter and sugar until light and fluffy.
2. Mix together the beaten egg, milk, and vanilla.
3. Add this gradually to the creamed butter mixture, stirring thoroughly.
4. Sift together the flour, baking powder, and salt.
5. Stir this into the mixture to make a stiff paste.
6. Roll out the paste on a lightly floured board.
7. Cut shapes with cookie cutters.
8. Place the cookies on an ungreased baking sheet and sprinkle the tops with sugar.
9. Bake at 375°F for 8 to 10 minutes.

4 Fruit salad: The simple activity of chopping fruit can be thoroughly absorbing for a four-year-old and will encourage a recognition of which fruits need peeling, and which need to have their pits or seeds removed, and so on.

5 Cookies and pastry tarts: Use cookie cutters, then decorate the shapes with cherries, raisins, icing, etc.

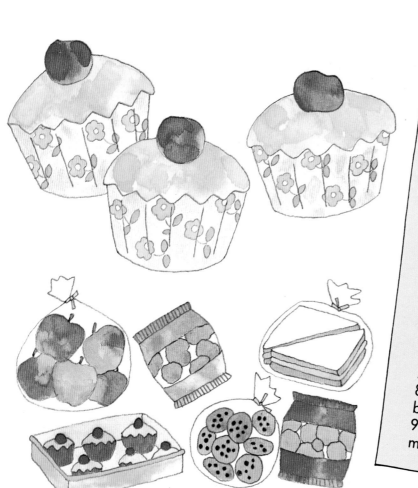

Cherry Muffins
10-15 candied cherries, chopped
1 cup flour
½ cup sugar
1 tsp baking powder
1 beaten egg
⅓ cup milk
2-4 tbsp melted butter

1. Fill a muffin tin with paper baking cups.
2. Wash the cherry pieces.
3. Sift the flour, salt, sugar, and baking powder.
4. Combine the butter and milk.
5. Add the egg and liquids to the dry ingredients.
6. Stir in the cherries.
7. Fill each baking cup ⅓ full.
8. Let your child scrape the bowl!
9. Bake at 400°F for 20-25 minutes.

Having a Picnic
Make a picnic and let your child choose the food. You don't have to go further than the living room to eat it. The fun is in preparing the snacks and packing the bags.

More about food

Where Does Food Come From?
Many children are surprised to learn that peas actually grow in pods on a plant, and that apples grow on trees, that carrots are roots, that milk comes from cows, and eggs from chickens.

Have some illustrations of animals, food, and food production in the kitchen when you are talking about food.

When you're cooking, let your child see the vegetables before you chop them up, and the meat or fish before you cook it.

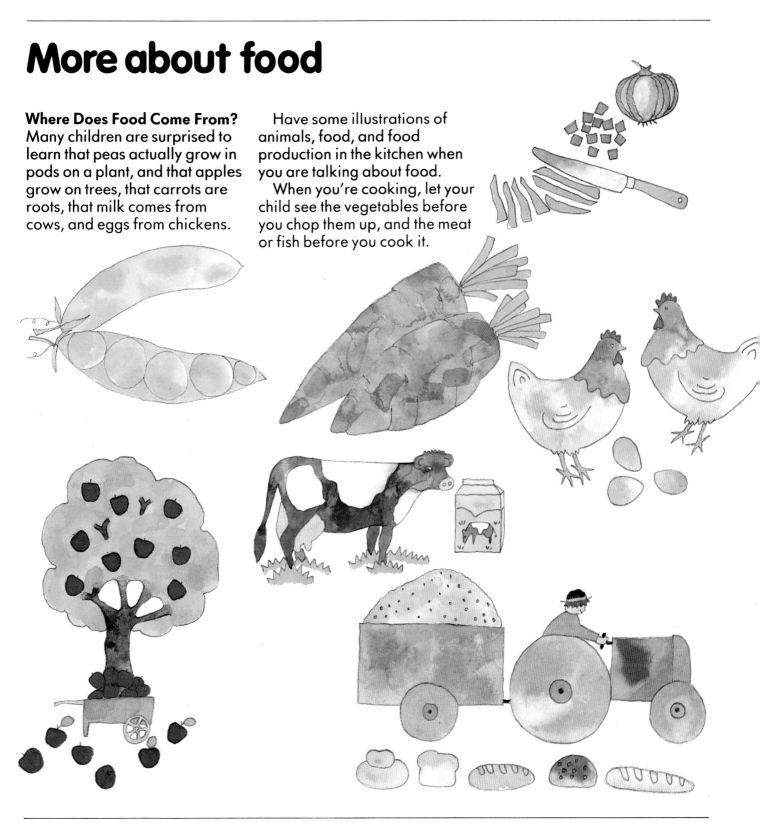

Know your body

Play games that will exercise all the different parts of your body, for example, stretching, bending, curling up, balancing. The game "Simon Says" is useful for this.

Sing these action songs, and act them out. If you don't know the tunes, make them up.

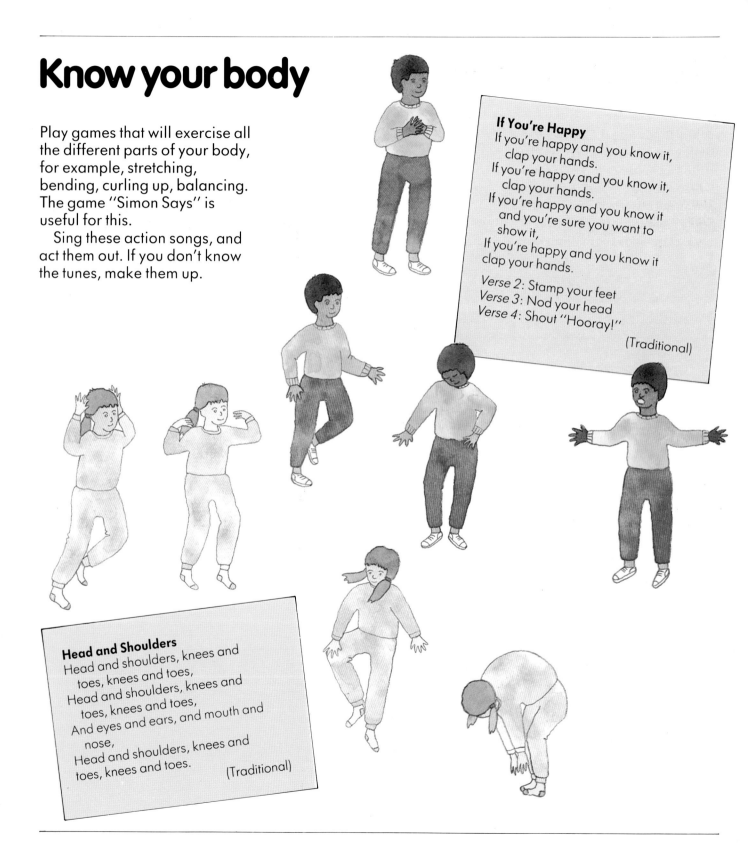

If You're Happy
If you're happy and you know it,
  clap your hands.
If you're happy and you know it,
  clap your hands.
If you're happy and you know it
  and you're sure you want to
  show it,
If you're happy and you know it
clap your hands.

Verse 2: Stamp your feet
Verse 3: Nod your head
Verse 4: Shout "Hooray!"

(Traditional)

Head and Shoulders
Head and shoulders, knees and
  toes, knees and toes,
Head and shoulders, knees and
  toes, knees and toes,
And eyes and ears, and mouth and
  nose,
Head and shoulders, knees and
  toes, knees and toes.

(Traditional)

Playing with water

Children love water and will take every opportunity to play with it. Put a board across the end of your bathtub and put some of the following items on it:

1. Squeeze bottles, milk cartons, and a plastic toy teapot (pierce holes in the sides of one of these). Use to make air bubbles and for pouring.

2. Pipes, metal rings, sprays, strainers, and funnels. Use by pouring water through them.

3. Lengths of tubing, such as plastic straws. Use to siphon water from one type of container to another.

4. Sponges, corks, spools, spoons, and plastic toys. Use for floating and sinking.

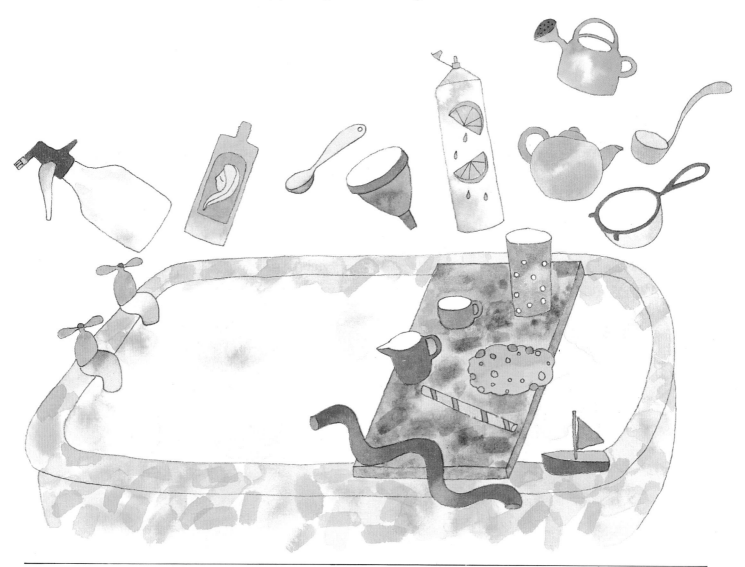

Water games

Water Games

1 Blowing detergent bubbles. Use plastic rings to blow through, or plastic straws cut diagonally at one end.

2 Add a few drops of cooking oil to a bowl of water and swirl it around to make patterns.

3 Playing with ice cubes. Watch them melt; drop them into cups of water and watch them float and crack.

4 Find two containers which hold the same amount of liquid but are different in shape—one taller and narrower than the other. Ask your child which holds the most water – the answer given will probably be the taller. Demonstrate that they both hold the same amount by filling them up and then pouring the water from each one in turn into a measuring cup.

Bottles of Water
Water in bottles,
Water in pans,
Water in kettles,
Water in cans—
It is always the shape
Of whatever it's in,
Bucket or kettle,
Or bottle or tin.

(Rodney Bennett)

Weighing

Make your own balance. Tie a margarine container to each end of a coat hanger. Make sure the pieces of string are equal in length and the tubs are hung at the same level. Hang up the hanger, using a longer piece of string.

Weigh a number of different items of varying sizes. You can then introduce words such as heavy, heavier, light and lighter.

Make sure that it is not always the larger objects which are heavy and the small ones which are light.

Using a Scale

Look at the weights given on food packages in the kitchen and check them on a set of scales.

Take two bowls. Weigh out 8 ounces of flour and place this in one bowl. Then weigh out 8 ounces of rice and put it in the other bowl. Which looks like the larger quantity, the flour or the rice?

Weigh out the same amounts of other ingredients, such as sugar, tomatoes, and peas. Compare the volume of these as well.

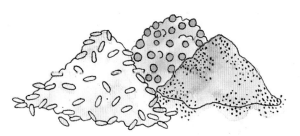

Out of doors

There is so much to see when you leave the house that it would be impossible to cover it all in one book. However, here are a few ideas:

1 Look carefully at construction sites. Can you see any cranes, pulleys, or wheels? How do they work? What is scaffolding used for?

2 Watch for garbage trucks, buses, fire engines, ambulances, cement mixers, cranes, police officers, and traffic lights. Talk about their jobs or functions.

3 Visit the local library, stores, and the post office.

4 Look for billboard advertisements, store names, road names, store door signs ("Push," "Pull," "Open," "Closed") and directions ("Exit," "Up," "Down"). Look, too, for symbols that replace words, such as those on road signs, arrows, and crossings.

5 When you get home, talk about what you have seen, using pictures and toys to help. For example: Look at the wheels and axles on toy cars.

Compare a police uniform with other uniforms. Which store would you go to, to buy objects seen in your home?

Lines and Squares
Whenever I walk in a London street,
I'm ever so careful to watch my
  feet;
And I keep in the squares,
And the masses of bears,
Who wait at the corners all ready
  to eat
The sillies who tread on the lines
  of the street
Go back to their lairs,
And I say to them, "Bears,
Just look how I'm walking in all
  the squares!"

And the little bears growl to each
  other, "He's mine,
As soon as he's silly and steps on
  a line."
And some of the bigger bears try to
  pretend
That they came round the corner to
  look for a friend;
And they try to pretend that nobody
  cares
Whether you walk on the lines or
  squares.
But only the sillies believe their
  talk;
It's ever so portant how you walk.
And it's ever so jolly to call out,
  "Bears,
Just watch me walking in all the
  squares!"

(A.A. Milne)

Things to collect

Tickets, store receipts, shells, colored pebbles, feathers, autumn leaves, twigs, pine cones, nuts, seeds, and berries (also a good moment to warn your child **not** to taste any berries and to wash his or her hands after touching them).

Using your Collections

1. Sort the objects and place into small boxes for display.

2. Use them to make collages and models.

3. Make prints by gently rubbing shoe polish onto the backs of leaves and then pressing the leaves onto a sheet of paper.

4 Divide the leaves into two groups—deciduous (from trees that shed their leaves in winter) and evergreens (from trees which keep their leaves throughout the winter).

5 Put some bare twigs into a vase to be used as stems for paper flowers. Or, loosely weave the twigs together by winding pieces of yarn around them to make a sculpture.

Lavender's Blue
Lavender's blue, dilly dilly,
Lavender's green,
When I am King, dilly, dilly,
You shall be Queen.

(Traditional)

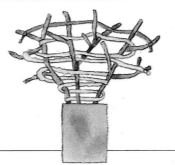

6 Take some flowers from the garden (do not pick wildflowers as many types of wildflower are now becoming extremely rare), and put them between pieces of blotting paper. Pile up some heavy books on top and leave the blossoms to press flat.

7 If you have roses in your garden, collect the petals from fading blooms and dry them. Crush them in a handkerchief or square of calico and tie up the corners with ribbon to make a scented sachet.

Learn about growing

Look at some seeds that have wings. Explain how the wind helps to spread them so the seeds can find a place to grow.

Illustrate how plants need water by putting some flowers into a clear vase and marking the water level each day.

Illustrate how plants need light by turning a young plant around and watching its shoots grow toward the light.

Cover one leaf on a plant with foil to cut it off from the light and see what happens.

Growing Beans
Line a glass jar with tissues or blotting paper. Place a few bean seeds between the glass and the paper so that you can see them through the sides of the glass. Fill the jar with water and keep it in a warm place. The beans will grow some roots first, and then shoots.

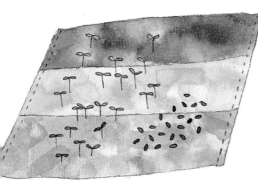

Growing Alfalfa Sprouts

Place a damp tissue or piece of cheesecloth in a saucer and sprinkle it with a few alfalfa seeds. Keep them damp and warm.

Think of some alternative pots for your alfalfa—you could use a margarine container, or even an eggshell—on which you could paint a face.

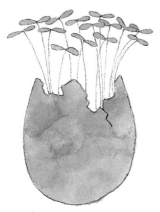

Root Vegetables

Cut off the top part of a carrot. Place the sliced edge in a shallow dish of water and watch it sprout new leaves from the top.

Mary, Mary
Mary, Mary, quite contrary,
How does your garden grow?
With silver bells and cockle shells
And pretty maids all in a row.

(Traditional)

Bean Sprouts

Put some dried mung beans in a jar and stretch a piece of cheesecloth firmly over the top. Soak the jar overnight in warm water, then drain and leave it in a sunny place. Keeping the cheesecloth in place, rinse the beans twice a day and watch them grow into bean sprouts. (The sprouts can be used in stir-fry dishes, or eaten cold in salads.)

What the Leaves Said
The leaves said, "It's autumn,
Aren't we all gay?"
Scarlet and golden
And russet were they.

The leaves said, "It's winter,
Where are we?"
So they lay down and slept
Under a tree.

The leaves said, "It's spring,
And here are we,
Opening and stretching
On every tree."

The leaves said, "It's summer,
Each bird has a nest,
We make the shadow
Where they can rest."

(Unknown)

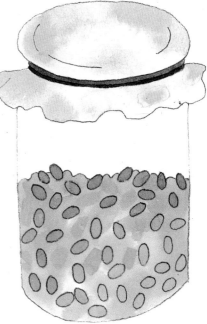

Animal homes

Look for holes, nests, and webs. But do not go too close if it seems as if the animal may still be using the home.

You may find a fox's den under tree roots; or a rabbit's burrow in a grassy bank. Look, too, for squirrels' nests in the branches of trees.

Look for birds' nests in trees and hedges. Don't disturb them during the spring or summer, but if you find an abandoned nest in the winter have a look to see how it is made. In the spring, you may also see birds flying to their nests with their beaks full of straw, tissue paper, and other nesting materials.

If you find a spiderweb, see if you can spot its owner lurking under a leaf by one corner. You may also see a "spider's nursery"—a tightly woven area of web between two grassy stalks where the spider's eggs are laid.

In the summer you may see "sponges" on the stems of plants and grass. Each white blob of froth is the home of a larva of an insect. It wraps the froth around itself for protection.

Feeding signs

Look for chewed pine cones and opened nuts on the ground under trees. Hazelnuts opened by squirrels are cracked in half, whereas mice nibble uneven holes in nuts to get at the kernel

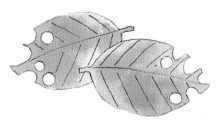

caterpillars and slugs. Look for leaves that have been chewed. Some leaves have white or brown markings winding over the surface. The markings are made by leaf miners (the grubs of moths or flies), which eat the leaves from inside.

Look, too, at animals and insects as they collect their food. For example, ducks dive head down to search through the weeds. Butterflies and bees gather nectar from flowers. Ants scurry back to their nest with bundles of food.

inside. You may also find a broken snail shell near a slab of stone. This would be left behind by a song thrush, who uses

stones to crack open the snail shells to get at the snail inside. Spiders, too, often leave behind the remains of flies unlucky enough to get caught in their webs.

Leaves provide food for many small creatures, such as

Keeping pets

The chance of looking after a living creature is very rewarding for young children. Not only do they learn about the animal and its life, but also how to care for it.

Some small wild animals and insects can be kept for a few days without much harm; for example, beetles, caterpillars, spiders, and worms. Keep them in containers which let in air, but will also prevent them from escaping. You can use small fish tanks or jars, sealed firmly with netting or paper covered with lots of pinholes.

Caterpillars
Caterpillars can be collected from hedges and the leaves of flowers throughout the summer. Remember not to remove them from the leaf on which you find them and to give them fresh leaves of the same kind every day.

After a while, the caterpillar will build itself a cocoon (called a chrysalis). Then, a couple of weeks later, it will emerge as a butterfly or moth and will want to fly away. Do not try to keep butterflies or moths or they will soon die.

Some caterpillars and most butterflies have beautiful markings. You could make a collage of a butterfly from tissue paper. To make the wings identical in size and design, paint the shape of one wing and then fold the paper in half before the paint dries (see opposite page).

The Centipede
The centipede was happy quite,
Until the toad in fun
Said, "Pray, which leg goes after which?"
Which worked his mind to such a pitch,
He lay distracted in a ditch,
Considering how to run.   (Unknown)

Tickle Rhyme
"Who's that tickling my back?"
Said the wall.
"Me," said the small caterpillar,
"I'm learning to crawl."

(Ian Serraillier)

Snails and Insects

Snails can be found under stones in fields or yards and on the side of walls during the summer. They should always be kept in a moist atmosphere—put some damp soil in the jar with them. Snails feed mainly at night, so give them some fresh green leaves each evening.

Insects can be found anywhere outdoors. They usually feed on leaves, mealy worms, and other bugs.

Spiders

Spiders can be caught in bushes or in the house. Scoop them up in a cardboard box so they are not harmed.

You can only keep a spider for a few days so it will not need feeding, but if you can trap a small fly it will provide the spider with a tasty meal.

Carefully place the spider in a jar that will give it plenty of room, with a little cup inside it containing wet cotton balls.

1. Draw a spiral pattern onto an 8 inch square wooden board.
2. Partially hammer 33 nails into the board as shown below.
3. Starting from the center and working outward, wind a piece of thread around each of the pins. Do not include the seven outer nails of the spiral.
4. Then wind the thread backward and forward across the outer nails on the board, as shown in the drawing, to make the radiating lines of the web.

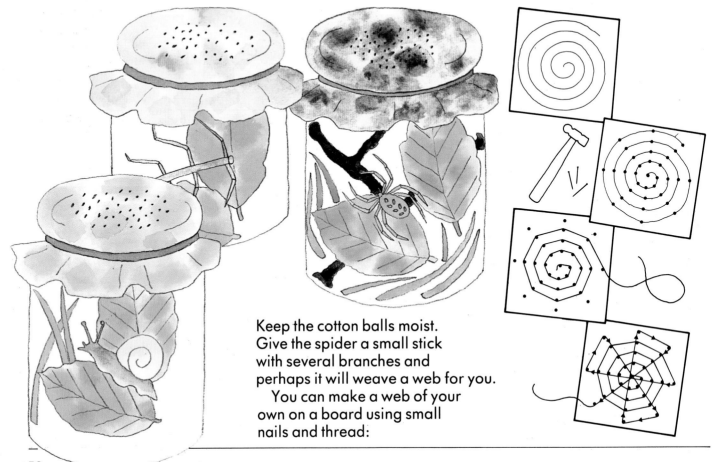

Keep the cotton balls moist. Give the spider a small stick with several branches and perhaps it will weave a web for you.

You can make a web of your own on a board using small nails and thread:

Whatever the weather

On a Sunny Day

1 To paint a large sun, splotch thick paint onto the center of a piece of paper and use fingers to paint the rays spreading outward.

2 Paint on the sidewalks with water, using painters' brushes.

3 How many things can you think of to cool you down—ice cream, ice cubes, cold baths, garden hoses . . . . .

4 Study your shadow. When is it shorter or longer? Does it always fall in the same direction? Watch it as you jump, run, dance, and pass other people.

Trace someone's shadow onto a large sheet of paper—or paint it in water on the sidewalk.

Rainbows

Rainbows are seen when the sun shines through drops of water.

1 Make your own by putting a glass of water on a windowsill. You will need a bright sunny day. Place the glass so that the edge just hangs over the edge of the sill. A rainbow should form on the floor. Or, stand with your back to the sun and look through the spray from a garden hose or sprinkler.

2 Cut a circle of cardboard. Divide the circle into seven parts, one for each color of the rainbow. Color each of the parts as shown in the drawing, and put a pencil through a hole in the middle. Now spin the card.

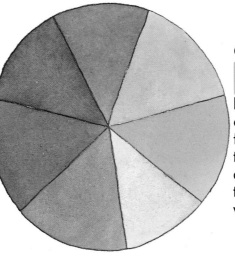

On a Cloudy Day

1 Make a picture of a cloudy sky using cotton balls glued to the paper for clouds. Develop the theme further by glueing scraps of thick material underneath and drawing heads and feet on them to represent people dressed in warm clothes.

2 Look at the different types of clouds. The wispy "Mares' tails" usually mean fine weather. Fluffy "Cumulus" clouds, which look like cotton balls, will mean fine weather if they are small or showers if they are large and gray. Huge patches or "blankets" of gray or white clouds ("Stratus" cloud) usually mean rain.

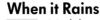

When it Rains

1 Hold a thin sheet of paper (so that the surface is flat) out of the window for a few seconds. Bring the paper inside, but keep it flat until the water it has caught has seeped through, then hold it up to a light to see the pattern of the raindrops.

When the Wind Blows

1 Watch the wind blowing the branches of trees, lifting kites, and moving smoke. How many other things can you see that are affected by the wind?

2 Go outside and hold up a wet finger—the side that becomes cold first is the side the wind blows from.

3 Watch the way the clouds move.

2 Talk about what happens to rivers when it rains. Where does all the rainwater from the roofs, roads, and hills go?

The seasons

Make large collage pictures to illustrate the seasons. Use your child's paintings as well as pictures from magazines, and objects like leaves, flower petals, and grass.

Tell stories about the seasons, for example, "Going for a walk in winter," "The park in summer," "What a squirrel does in the fall," "The robin in springtime."

Bring out the different features of each season in your stories. For example, in the fall talk about blackberries, squirrels gathering nuts, leaves falling, fog, bonfires.

In winter, talk about animals going into hibernation, frost, snow, bare twigs, long nights, rosy cheeks, Christmas, warm clothes, fires.

In spring—new shoots, crocuses, daffodils, Easter eggs, umbrellas for showers.

In summer—long days, bees, flowers, strawberries, picnics, trips to the beach, swimwear, wading pools, playing outdoors.

Rain
There are holes in the sky
Where the rain gets in
But they're ever so small
That's why rain is so thin.
(Spike Milligan)

Go Wind Blow
Go wind blow,
Push wind, swoosh.
Shake things, take things,
Make things fly.
Ring things, swing things,
Fling things high.
Go wind blow,
Push wind . . . . . whee!
No wind, no!
Not me, not me!
(from "Play School")

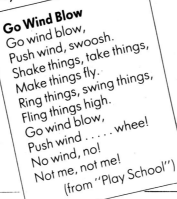

What to wear

1 Take out a variety of clothes and talk about which clothes are suitable for which kinds of weather. Sort them into piles for summer wear and winter wear, or a trip to the beach, or a winter vacation.

2 Make paper clothes for all weathers to dress up cardboard dolls.

3 Look at pictures of animals' fur and birds' feathers—which animals grow thicker fur in winter? Drop a little water onto a feather to see how waterproof it is.

4 Cover three wooden play blocks with white paper, or make three cardboard cubes (see diagram on page 87). On the first cube draw six heads—one on each side. On the second, draw six upper bodies and arms; and on the third, six lower bodies and legs.

Vary the clothing in each drawing to make up six people wearing six different outfits. For example: Cotton dress and sun hat, Eskimo type furs, swimsuit and flippers, a uniform, boots and raincoat, working overalls.

Match the correct sides to make up the whole characters, and mix them up, too.

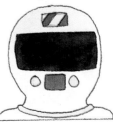

Matching
and Numbers

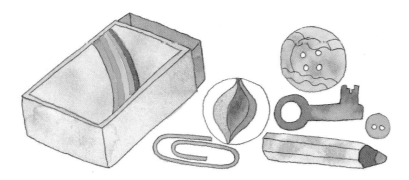

Color

1 Sort any group of objects into piles according to color. For example, divide the laundry into dark and light clothes.

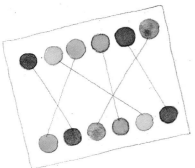

2 Paint six different colors on the left-hand side of a piece of paper and then put the same colors in a different order on the opposite side. Then match up the colors by connecting them with a pencil line. (Encourage your child to work from left to right as a preparation for reading.)

3 Draw two rows of six circles. Color in the top six yourself but leave the others for your child to color in matching shades.

4 Collect pictures from magazines. Cut a piece of color from each picture. Mount the pictures onto cardboard and match the colored piece to the correct picture.

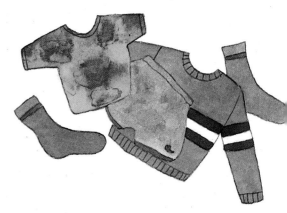

A color game

Make a spinner out of a piece of cardboard (see page 87) and divide it into six colors. Or, cover the six sides of a square wooden block with a different color for each side. Then divide a large sheet of stiff cardboard into 20 squares. Color in all the squares using the six colors on the spinner or block. (Or, you can buy packets of gummed colored squares and glue these onto the cardboard instead.) Mark the "Start" and "Finish" boxes and glue or paint on a few arrows to show which direction the players can move. You will also need some counters.

To play—spin the spinner or use the block like a die, and move your counter to the next square matching the color the spinner has stopped on. The winner is the first person to reach the "Home" square by spinning the correct color.

To make the game more fun, you could paste on some snakes and ladders as well. When a player reaches a square containing a snake's head, he or she must move back to the square at the end of its tail. If a player lands on a square at the bottom of a ladder, he or she may go forward to the square at the top of the ladder.

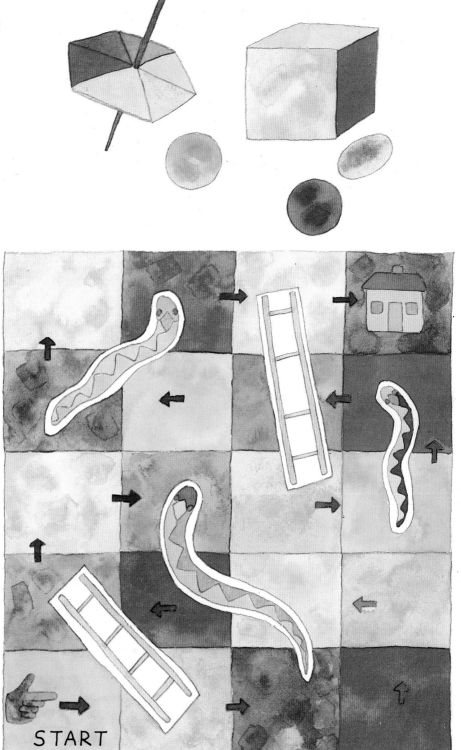

START

Shapes

1 Cut a piece of fruit in half and point out how each half matches in shape.

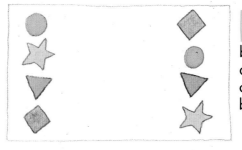

2 Fold a long piece of paper into pleats not less than 2 inches wide. Cut the pleated paper into any shape, but be careful to leave some of the edges on both sides uncut. Open out the paper and you should have a row of identical shapes.

3 Paste some simple shapes onto the left-hand side of a piece of paper (you can buy boxes of gummed paper shapes, or see page 77 for some examples which you could trace). Paste the same shapes, but in a different order, onto the opposite side of the paper, and connect the identical shapes with pencil lines.

4 Find an example of each of the solid shapes shown below and say what the names of the shapes are. Now look for other objects that have similar basic shapes.

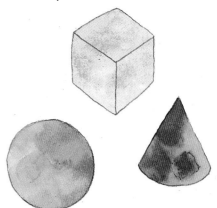

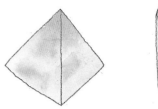

5 Draw four objects onto a piece of cardboard. Make them very different in shape—for example, a pencil, a bottle, a cereal box, and a ball. Cut the pictures out. Now make four cards, each one showing a container that fits the shape of each of the objects. Make the shapes very simple, so that it will be easy for your child to match the container to the object.

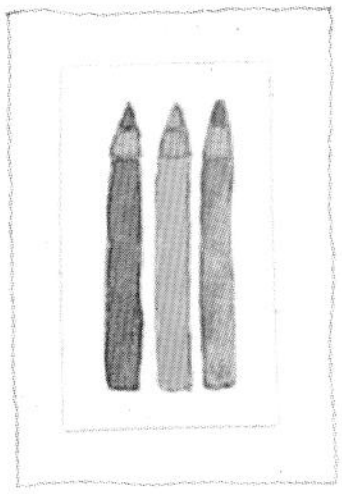

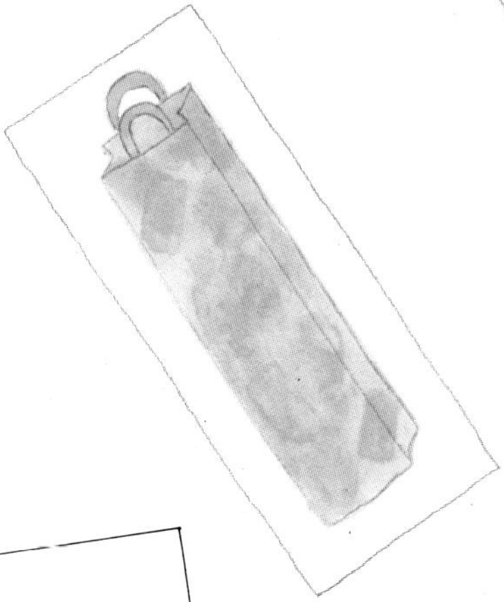

Two Little Dicky Birds
Two little dicky birds,
Sitting on the wall,
One named Peter,
The other named Paul.
Fly away Peter, fly away Paul.
Come back Peter, come back Paul.

(Traditional)

Sizes

Does your child understand words that indicate size, such as big, large, small, short, tall, and long? Draw or glue pairs of pictures onto a large piece of paper to demonstrate the meaning of big and little, long and short, fat and thin. Talk about the pictures and put circles around the smallest, shortest and thinnest.

1 Make two cards—one bigger and one smaller. Write the words "bigger" and "smaller" on the cards to help beginner readers. Make each word clearly match the size of the card.

Now take two objects that are the same shape, but different sizes, such as a tablespoon and a teaspoon. Put the tablespoon on the "bigger" card, and the teaspoon on the "smaller" card. Use a variety of other objects as well, for example, a basketball and tennis ball, a quarter and a dime, a big bowl and a small bowl. Sometimes put the smaller object down first, and sometimes the bigger, and put each pair down separately.

2 Collect several cans or jars of different sizes, each one with a lid. Take the lids off and mix them up. Put the right lid back on the right pot.

3 Collect a number of small objects and sort them into two piles—those that you think will fit into a matchbox and those that won't. Now find an empty matchbox and see if you are right.

4 Take a selection of toys and other objects and sort them into two piles—those that you think would fit through a mailbox and those that won't. Cut a hole the size of a mail slot into the side of a cardboard box. Now try "mailing" the things in your pile.

This game can also be played using holes of different shapes and sizes.

5 Line up a row of books of different heights on a flat piece of wood, or tabletop. Now arrange them in order of height.

Games to play

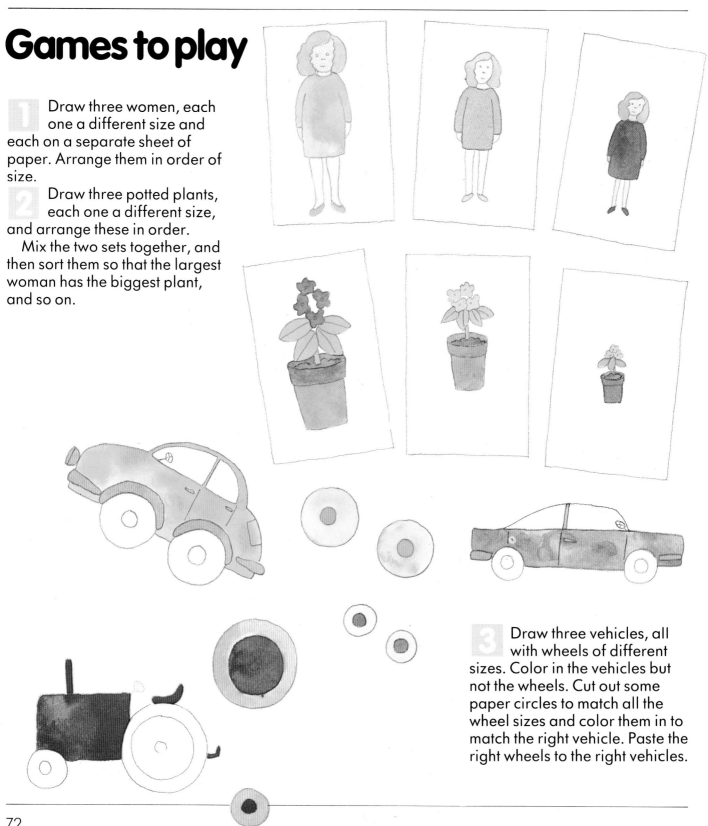

1 Draw three women, each one a different size and each on a separate sheet of paper. Arrange them in order of size.

2 Draw three potted plants, each one a different size, and arrange these in order.

Mix the two sets together, and then sort them so that the largest woman has the biggest plant, and so on.

3 Draw three vehicles, all with wheels of different sizes. Color in the vehicles but not the wheels. Cut out some paper circles to match all the wheel sizes and color them in to match the right vehicle. Paste the right wheels to the right vehicles.

Goldilocks and the three bears

Cut a sheet of cardboard into 12 pieces. Draw each of the bears on three of the cards, their chairs on three others, their porridge bowls on three others, and their beds on the last three. Each time, make one of the drawings large, one medium-sized, and one small. Tell the story, holding up the cards as illustrations. Then play with the cards, sorting them by object and then by size.

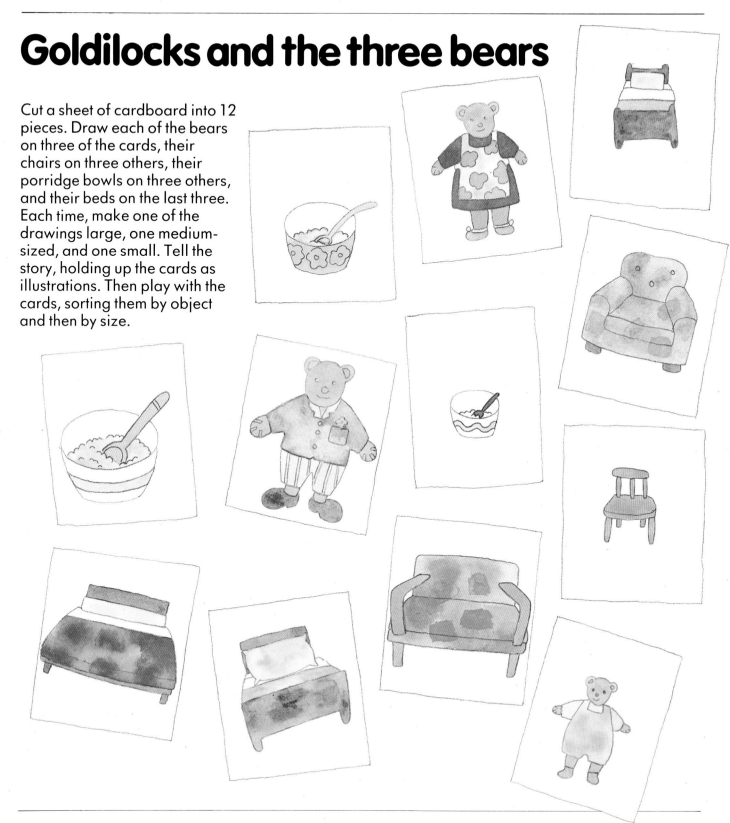

Things that go together

Shape Matching

Cut out some cardboard templates of basic shapes (some examples are on page 77). Make up some pictures by drawing around the templates on a clean piece of paper. To complete the designs, give your child some ready-made shapes cut out from gummed colored paper.

To make a game from this project, make up a few pictures on separate pieces of cardboard using the outlines of only six different shapes. Then cut out a set of all the shapes needed to complete all the pictures and color them in. Make a die from a piece of firm cardboard (see page 87) with each shape shown on one side of the die.

Each player is given an outline picture.

The colored shapes are spread out randomly over the table.

To play—the first player throws the die. If the shape that falls uppermost on the die matches one on his or her outline picture, the player picks up the matching piece from the colored shapes and places it on their card. The winner is the first person to complete a picture.

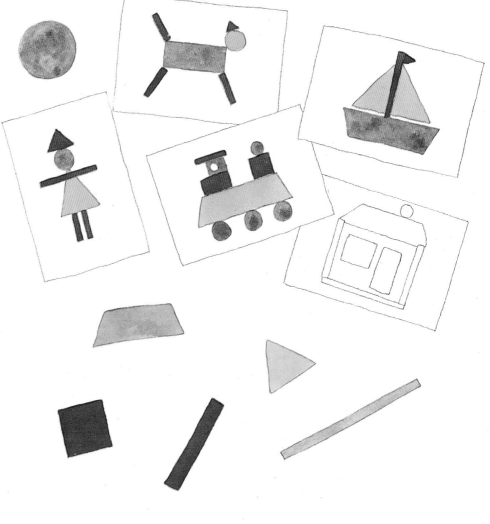

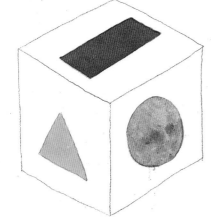

Shadow Matching

Glue 12 clearly outlined pictures onto thick cardboard and cut them out. (Inexpensive coloring books are a good source for these kinds of pictures.) Take another piece of card and trace around each cut-out. Color in the shapes with black. Now match the cut-out pictures to the shadow shapes.

Picture Pairs

Build up a collection of pictures of things that can be paired, such as a spider and its web, a telephone and its receiver, and so on. Mix up all the pictures and then sort them into the correct pairs. You can also do this with real objects—like a knife and fork, cup and saucer, hairbrush and comb, etc.

Mix and match

1 Make some cards showing the two halves of different pictures, for example, the heads and tails of animals or the tops and bottoms of buildings. Jumble up all the cards, then match up the halves.

2 Gather an assortment of shoes, boots, and slippers; or cut out pictures of shoes from magazines and mount them onto separate bits of cardboard. Now sort them into pairs, colors, or types.

Making your own cards

Cards can be used for all kinds of matching and pairing games. Whether you use letters, numbers, or pictures on your cards depends on your child's knowledge and ability. Choose simple shapes and pictures for a young child, and clearly written numbers, letters, and simple words for a child learning to count and read.

There are some suggestions for games on the following pages, but first, here are a few general hints about making cards.

Recommended card size
Make your cards about 3 inches by 2¼ inches—for dominoes these can easily be divided in half.

Designs

1 Shapes—use the shapes shown on the previous page by tracing over them.

2 Pictures—the pictures shown on the next few pages will give you some ideas.

3 Numbers—use only the numbers from 0 to 10 to begin with and write them out clearly.

4 Letters—use lower case (i.e., small) letters only to begin with, and write them out clearly and boldly.

5 Words (for playing Snap) —choose words that your child is learning and use lower case letters throughout.

Color Coding

To help your child match up the cards you could use color coding. For example, make all the cards in one set the same color, and all the cards in another set a different color.

Other Uses

When you are making cards for a particular game, think of other ways in which they can be used. For example, choose pictures that can be grouped together, such as shoes and socks or hats and coats. Or draw objects that illustrate the words your child is learning to read.

All of the games mentioned on the next three pages can be played using either shape, picture, number, or letter cards.

Card games

Pairs
Make a set of 12 pairs of cards (24 cards in all). Scatter them face down on the table.

To play—the first player turns over any two cards. If they are a pair the player picks them up and keeps them. If not, the player must turn them face down again, leaving them in the same position (and trying to remember what was on them). Then it is the turn of the next player. The winner is the person to collect the most pairs.

For young children: To introduce the game to a young child, use only three pairs (six cards) to begin with and gradually increase the number of pairs.

Lotto

This game is for two players. Make 12 pairs of cards (24 in all). Put one card from each pair in a box and shake them up. Lay six of the other cards face up in front of each player.

To play—each player in turn chooses a card from the box. If the card they have chosen matches one of the cards in front of them they place it on top of the correct card. If not, the card is returned to the box. The winner is the first person to cover the six cards.

Happy Families

Make 24 cards—six sets with four identical cards in each set. Shuffle the cards and deal six to each player. Stack the remainder face down between the players. The object is to collect complete sets of four identical cards.

To play—the first player asks another player for a card (to match one that he holds in his hand). For example, one player could ask another one for a card with a cat on it.

If the other player has the card she must hand it over immediately to the first player, who then has another turn. If the other player doesn't have the card, the first player takes a card from the stack in the center and the turn passes to the next player. When a player completes a set, he or she should place it on the table.

The game continues until all the sets have been collected. The winner is the player with the largest number of sets.

Snap

Make 24 cards—six sets with four identical cards in each set. Shuffle the cards and deal them all out among the players, face downward so that the players do not know what cards they have.

To play—each player in turn takes a card from the top of his pack and places it face up on the table. When two identical cards appear together both players must shout "snap!" The first player to call out wins all the cards that have been put down so far and adds them to the bottom of her own pile.

The winner is either the player who has the most cards at the end of the game, or the one who wins all the cards.

Note: For games of Snap or Happy Families involving more than two players, you may wish to make more than six sets of cards.

The meaning of numbers

Make use of everyday opportunities to help your child understand the meaning of numbers and how numbers are used.

For example, when setting the table you could:

1 Talk about what "one" represents, such as "One knife for Mom," "One knife for Dad," and so on.

2 Compare stacks of plates of different sizes.

3 Show how numbers of objects have nothing to do with size of objects. For example, is four of something always the same size? Try carrying in four teaspoons and then four chairs.

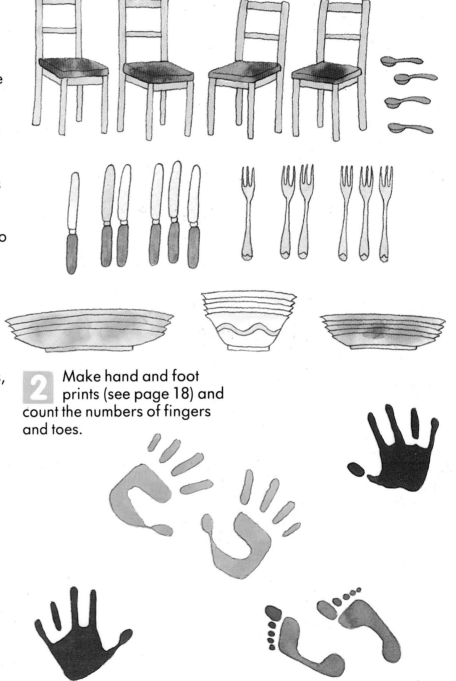

Counting

1 Count out piles of buttons, rice, raisins, or similar objects into plastic plates or cups.

2 Make hand and foot prints (see page 18) and count the numbers of fingers and toes.

3 Make "counting pictures," for example, lights on a Christmas tree, peas in a pod, a flock of birds, eggs in a nest, wheels on a train.

5 Place three buttons on a table. Ask your child to put three other objects next to them. Repeat this project with all the numbers that your child is learning.

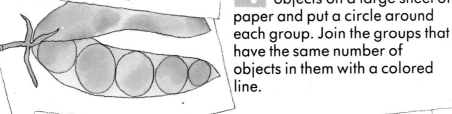

4 Draw different groups of objects on a large sheet of paper and put a circle around each group. Join the groups that have the same number of objects in them with a colored line.

Picture Chart
Count all the people or vehicles passing your window during the space of, say, five or ten minutes. Draw a picture chart to show how many there were of each kind.

Jumping Jack

Make a hinged cardboard figure (see pages 100–101).

Draw a picture of a wide river with steppingstones across it. Make the puppet "jump" from stone to stone and count the jumps.

Or, put some newspaper steppingstones on the floor so that your child can count his or her own jumps.

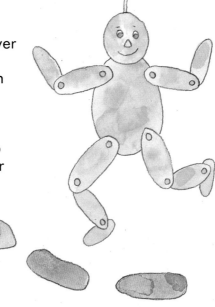

More or Less

Introduce the words "more" and "less."

1 Place some buttons in a row of plastic trays in numerical sequence, i.e. one button in the first tray, two in the second, three in the third, etc.

By pointing to each tray from left to right, show that there is one more button in each tray. Then do the same thing but in the reverse sequence. (If you don't have enough buttons use nuts or pebbles or something similar.)

2 Make a selection of picture cards showing groups of objects from one to four. These can be arranged in various ways, showing cards going from low numbers to high, from high to low, or different groups of the same numbers.

3 Draw the outlines of two groups of objects with a different number of objects in each group. Help your child to color in, say, the larger group in red and the smaller in blue.

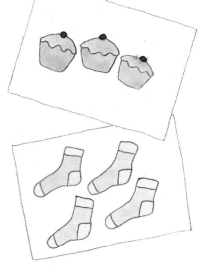

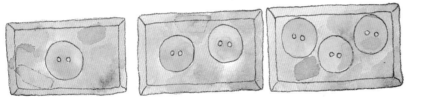

Number games

Number Dominoes
Make a set of domino cards following the sequence shown below. Use dots to represent the numbers and only do the numbers from 1 to 6. Make your cards more interesting by making a picture out of the dots, like the butterfly shown here.

To play—place all dominoes face down on one side of the table. Each player takes eight dominoes. The first player lays down one domino face up. If the second player has a matching domino they put that domino down. If not, they take a domino from the spare pile. The winner is the first to play all their dominoes.

Jigsaw Game
Mount six pictures onto thick cardboard, then divide each picture into six pieces. Clearly number each piece from one to six—using dots, not figures. Make a die (see page 87). For two players use two of the pictures, for three players use three pictures, and so on.

Show each player one completed jigsaw picture, then mix up all the pieces and place them all face upward in the middle of the table. The aim is for the players to collect the six pieces required to complete their picture.

To play—each player in turn shakes the die and finds the piece from his or her picture that corresponds to the number shown on the die. The winner is the first person to complete a picture.

1	1		1	2		1	3		1	4		1	5		1	6
			2	2		2	3		2	4		2	5		2	6
						3	3		3	4		3	5		3	6
									4	4		4	5		4	6
												5	5		5	6
															6	6

Board games

Make some simple board games. They can represent either:

1 A single winding track, such as the route home from school, a treasure hunt, or a maze.

2 Parallel tracks, such as a race track or railroad tracks.

3 Adjacent squares, such as a "snakes and ladders" game (see page 67).

Keep the games fairly simple and try to work in jokes,

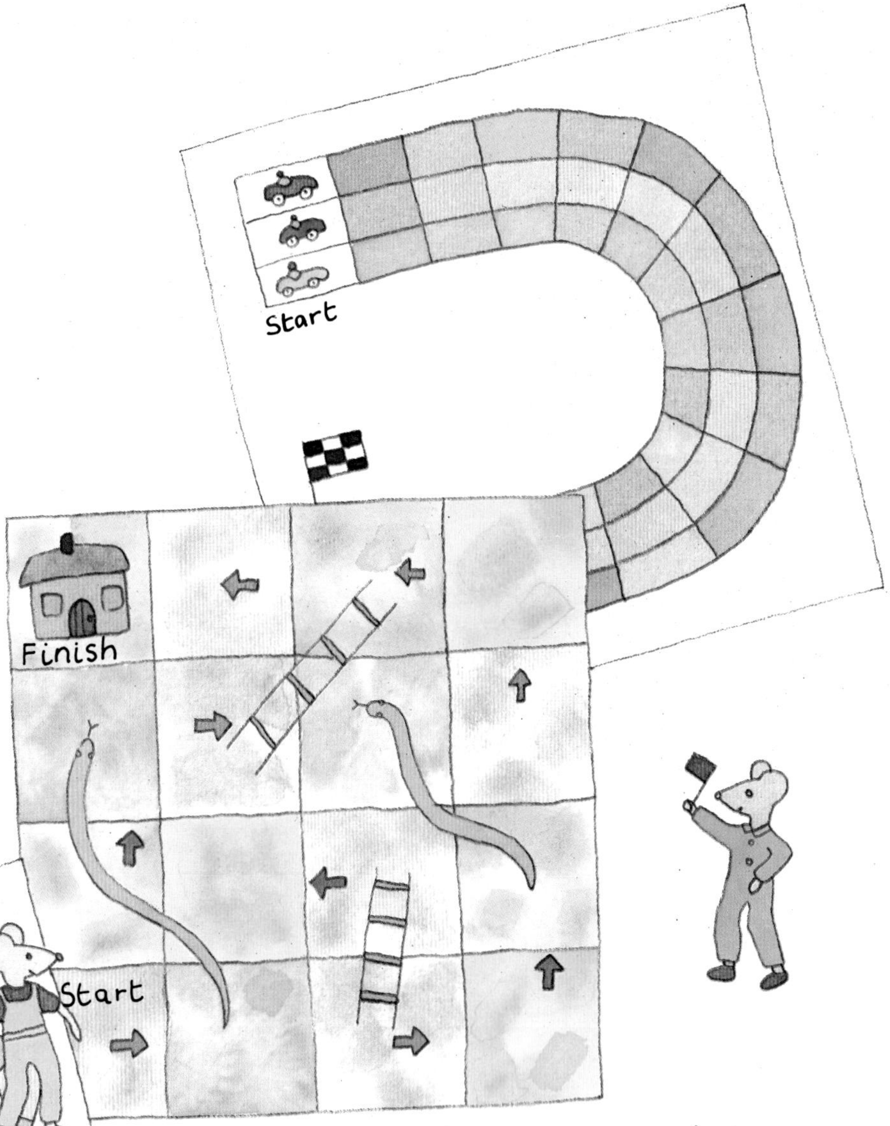

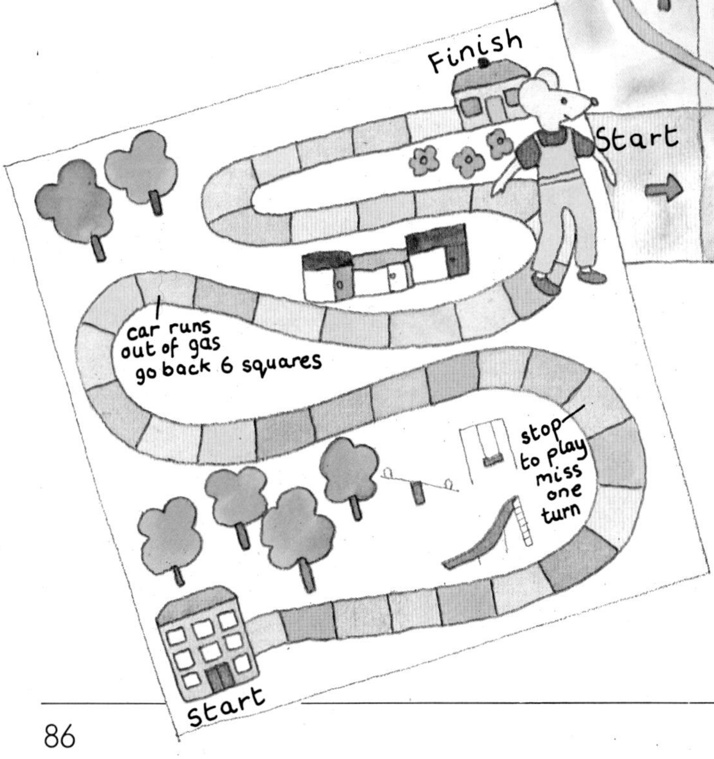

Start

Finish

Finish

Start

car runs out of gas go back 6 squares

stop to play miss one turn

Start

characters, or pets that your family all know.

The games can serve as either simple counting exercises or as lessons in reading and understanding the instructions given on the boards.

Use colored counters, and make your own die or spinner (as shown on the next page).

Making dice and spinners

To Make a Die

Trace around the diagram shown here. Cut out this shape from firm cardboard and color in the dots in the sequence shown.

Fold along all the dotted lines. Then glue the flaps to the sides with the matching letters—in alphabetical order—for example, flap "a" to side "a" and so on.

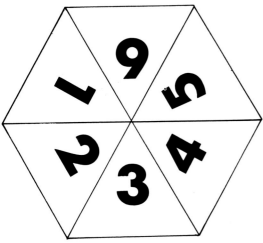

To Make a Spinner

Trace around the diagram shown here. Cut the hexagon shape from thick cardboard. Draw on the lines and the numbers (or use dots instead of numbers). Push a toothpick or a pencil with a sharp point through the center of the hexagon and spin it between thumb and index finger.

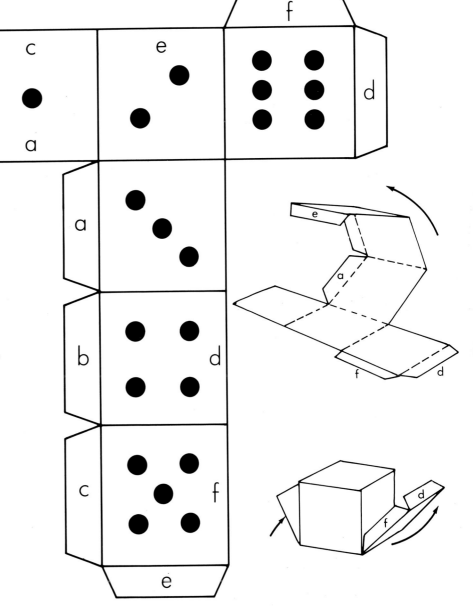

Number rhymes

The following number rhymes are just a few of the many that can be found in children's books. Where you can, act them out with your fingers while saying them.

You could also make up your own rhymes, for example:

1 2 3 4 Stephen's on the
   kitchen floor,
5 6 7 8 counting cookies on
   his plate.

Or, using the tune of "A Hundred Bottles of Beer on the Wall," change the words:

Ten pictures of me on the wall,
Ten pictures of me,
If one of those pictures should
   happen to fall,
Nine pictures of me on the
   wall . . . .

And so on.

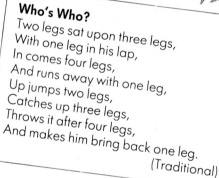

Buckle My Shoe
One, two, buckle my shoe,
Three, four, knock at the door,
Five, six, pick up sticks,
Seven, eight, shut the gate,
Nine, ten, a big fat hen.

(Traditional)

Who's Who?
Two legs sat upon three legs,
With one leg in his lap,
In comes four legs,
And runs away with one leg,
Up jumps two legs,
Catches up three legs,
Throws it after four legs,
And makes him bring back one leg.

(Traditional)

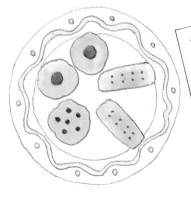

The Poor Widow
Here's to the poor widow from
   Babylon,
With six poor children all alone.
One can bake and one can brew,
One can shape and one can sew,
One can sit at the fire and spin,
One can bake a cake for the king.
Come choose you east, come choose
   you west,
Come choose the one that you
   love best.

(Traditional)

Ten Little Soldiers

Ten little soldiers
   Standing in a line,
One toddled home,
   And then there were nine.

Nine little soldiers
   Swinging on a gate,
One tumbled off,
   And then there were eight.

Eight little soldiers,
   Try to fly to heaven,
One lost his wings,
   And then there were seven.

(and so on, through the next verses)
Seven . . . Playing silly tricks,
   One broke his neck,
Six . . . . . . Kicking all alive,
   One went to bed,
Five . . . . On a cellar door,
   One tumbled in,
Four . . . . Out on a spree,
   One got sick,
Three . . . Out in a canoe,
   One tumbled overboard,
Two . . . . Fooling with a gun,
   One shot the other,

One little soldier,
   With his little wife,
Lived in a castle,
   The rest of his life.

(Traditional)

How Many?
3 young rats with black felt
   hats,
3 young ducks with white straw
   hats,
3 young dogs with curling
   tails,
3 young cats with demi veils,
Went out to walk with 2 young
   pigs,
In satin vests and sorrel wigs,
But suddenly it chanced to rain,
And so they all went home again.

(Traditional)

Recognizing and writing numbers

When your child seems to have a fairly clear idea of what numbers mean, you could help him or her to learn the symbols that represent the numbers.

Draw out the numbers your child knows in dotted lines so they can be traced over.

Number Jigsaws

Cut out ten cards. Write one of the numbers from one to ten on the top of each card and glue on or draw a group of simple objects of the same number below it.

Cut a wavy line between the number and picture on each card. Make sure the line is different for each one, to help your child match up the right picture with the right number.

Number Frieze

Fold up a long piece of paper, or stick a number of sheets together to make a frieze. Write the numbers from one to ten on the top of each sheet or folded section. Then stick pictures (or the objects themselves if they are light enough) underneath the numbers to illustrate each one.

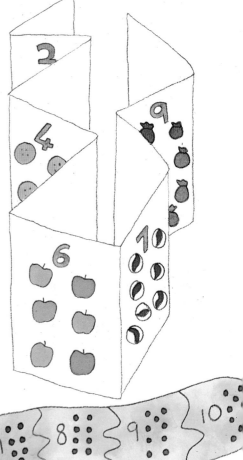

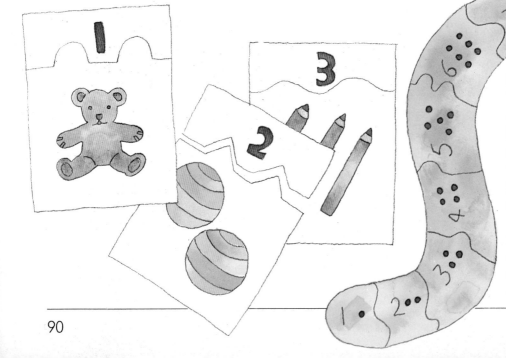

Number Worm

Take a piece of thick cardboard and draw a long wavy worm on it. Split the worm into ten segments and write the numbers from one to ten on each segment with the equivalent number of dots beside each number.

As you cut the segments up, make the curves of each cut different, so that the worm can only be reassembled with the numbers in the correct order.

Use practical examples to illustrate numbers to your child and, whenever possible, use real objects rather than pictures. For example:

Counting

1 "Let's do up your buttons—one, two, three . . ."

2 "How many people will be eating supper?" . . . "Here are all the knives and forks" . . . "How many forks have you got . . . can you give everyone a fork?" . . . "How many knives have you got . . . can you give everyone a knife?" . . . and so on, with spoons and dishes.

Adding On

1 "Here are two buttons . . . here are two more . . . how many are there now?"

2 "I have three pencils . . . pass me one more pencil . . . how many do I have now?"

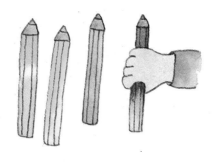

Taking Away

1 "There are five crackers on this plate. You eat one. How many are there now?"

2 "You have three dolls. If you give one doll to me, how many do you have left?"

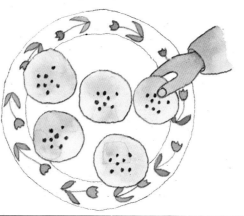

Sharing

"Here are four cupcakes. How many people are there in the room? Will they each be able to have a cupcake?"

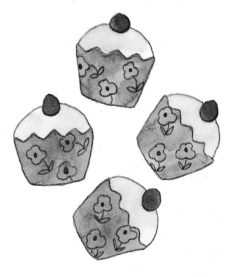

Shopping Games

You can buy and sell items around the house, such as toys, clothes, or groceries, using buttons, counters, or beans as money. Let one button represent one unit of money, such as one penny, so that there is no need to give change.

You could also collect a cupful of real pennies and play with them in the same way.

Measuring

Introduce these words wherever possible, and make some cards that you can ask questions about to help illustrate their meaning: high—highest, low—lowest, big—biggest, small—smallest, many, most, less.

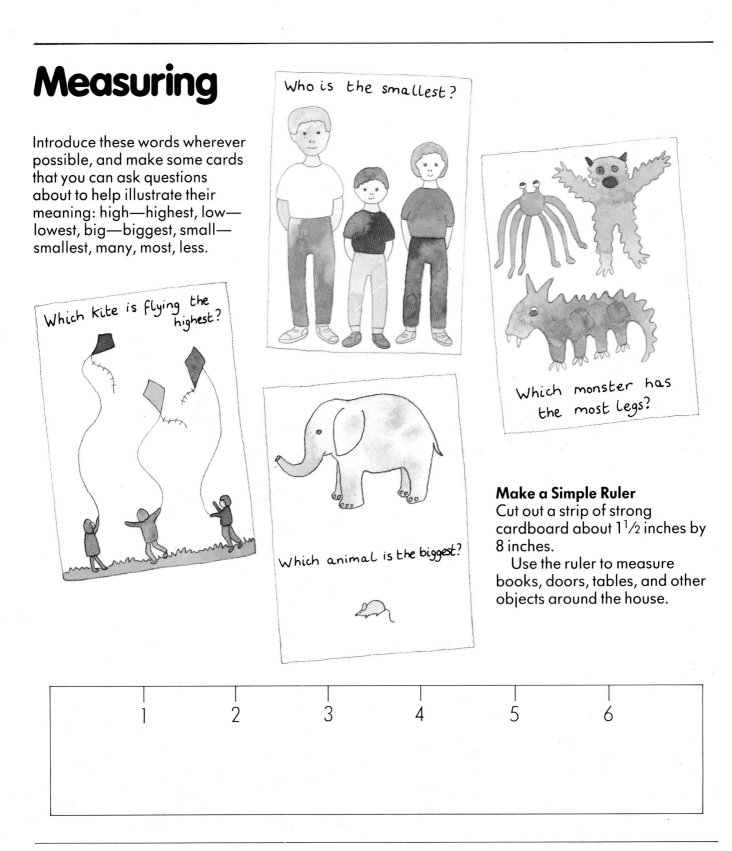

Who is the smallest?

Which kite is flying the highest?

Which animal is the biggest?

Which monster has the most legs?

Make a Simple Ruler
Cut out a strip of strong cardboard about 1½ inches by 8 inches.

Use the ruler to measure books, doors, tables, and other objects around the house.

| 1   2   3   4   5   6 |

Wordplay

Learning to listen

1 Hide a loudly ticking clock, or a transistor radio with the volume turned down, and see how quickly your child can find it.

2 Ask your child to close his or her eyes and listen to a sound that you will make, then try to guess correctly what the sound is. For example, you could shake a rattle, ring a bell, wind a clock or set off the alarm, jingle keys, tap fingers, rustle paper, close a door.

3 Both of you close your eyes and listen to sounds inside the room, or sounds you can hear outside. Talk about what you can hear and try to reproduce some of the sounds vocally and, later, with instruments.

4 Another day, both of you could try to reproduce sounds that your child knows well. For example, try the sound of footsteps, creaking or banging doors, a crying baby, the wind, a train, bees, a car, a clock ticking, the telephone.

5 Talk about the different types of sounds. What happens to the noise made by a motorcycle as it approaches and goes away? Can you reproduce this sound?

Things That Go "Bump"
Things that go "bump" in the night,
Should not really give one a fright.
It's the hole in each ear
That lets in the fear,
That, and the absence of light!

(Spike Milligan)

Making instruments

Make your child's first instruments from objects lying around the house. Use them to accompany any poems and songs you know.

Percussion Instruments

1 Drums: Use upturned pans, plastic bowls, empty boxes, or cans—cover the tops with waxed paper, or thick plastic, pulled tight and smooth and held in place by a thick rubber band.

2 Drumsticks: Use spoons, spools glued onto sticks, brushes, wire whisks.

3 Shakers: To introduce the idea, put some lentils, rice, pins, or buttons into matchboxes. Then ask your child to guess which matchboxes contain which objects by shaking them. Experiment with different fillings and containers.

4 Japanese drums: Take a small, round empty food box (a wooden box makes the best sound). Push a stick through a hole in the side of the box and tape it to the inside of the bottom so that it acts as a handle. Make two more holes in the sides of the box and thread two pieces of string through the holes (with a knot on the inside to hold them). Tie a bead to the end of each string, and tape the lid on securely. Shake the box so that the beads bang against the sides.

5 Bells: Use a bunch of keys, or a string of metal bottle tops. Thread some bottle tops onto a string and fasten them to a thick piece of wood (such as a piece of broom handle). Or, you could nail some individual tops loosely to the wood and bang the end on the ground so the tops ring.

6 Hanging bells: Hang anything metallic—nails, forks, foil dishes—or different sized clay flowerpots from separate pieces of string. Tap them with a spoon or some other form of drumstick.

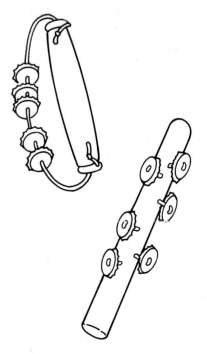

7 Cymbals: Use pairs of saucepan lids.

8 Castanets: Tape two spoons loosely together, as shown in the picture. Hold the handles firmly, and lightly tap out a rhythm on the palm of your free hand with the bowls of the spoons. Alternatively, take a strip of firm cardboard about 1½ inches by 8 inches, fold it in half, and glue a metal bottle top to the inside of the two ends. With one hand, tap the bottle tops together.

Jingle Bells
Jingle bells, jingle bells,
Jingle all the way,
Oh what fun it is to ride,
In a one-horse open sleigh!
(Traditional)

9 Xylophone: Pour some water into a row of glasses or empty bottles, varying the level of the water in each one. Tap the sides lightly with a metal spoon and listen to the sound made by each. Experiment with the pitch by increasing and decreasing the water levels.

10 Woodblocks: Any two pieces of wood that can be banged or rubbed together will do. Stick a smaller piece of wood onto the back of each one as handles. For an interesting effect, cover one side of each block with sandpaper and scrape one block across the other. Compare the noises made by different sized pieces of wood.

Wind Instruments

1 Trumpets: The simplest form of trumpet is a cardboard tube which you hum through, or a semicircle of cardboard rolled up to form a cone-shaped trumpet. Or, you could blow across the tops of empty plastic bottles.

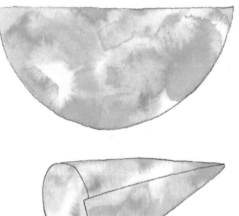

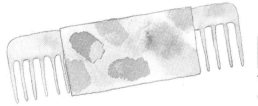

2 "Kazoo" comb: Fold a sheet of tissue paper over a large toothed comb. Press lips firmly against comb and tissue and hum.

Stringed Instruments

1 Double bass: Make two small holes (one at each end) in the bottom of a large, upturned cardboard box. Make some small cuts radiating out from one of the holes in the shape of a star. Push a broom handle through this hole and thread a piece of elastic through the other hole. Knot the end of the elastic inside the box and tie the other end to the top of the pole. Hold the pole firmly and pluck the elastic.

2 Zither: Stretch several rubber bands of different thicknesses around an open cardboard box and pluck. Make some small notches in the ends of the box to help to keep the rubber bands in place.

Alternatively, hammer a row of nails across one side of a rectangular piece of wood. Place another row of nails on the other side, directly opposite to the nails in the first row, but gradually decreasing the distance between the rows. Join each pair of nails with a taut rubber band and pluck.

Old King Cole
Old King Cole was a merry old soul,
And a merry old soul was he.
He called for his pipe,
And he called for his bowl,
And he called for his fiddlers three.

Now every fiddler he had a fiddle,
And a very fine fiddle had he,
Twee-tweedle-dee, tweedle-dee,
went the fiddlers.
Oh there's none so rare,
As can compare
With King Cole and his fiddlers three!

(Traditional)

Playacting with puppets

Puppets can be used to act out all kinds of simple rhymes and poems, and are a wonderful way of encouraging children to make up stories of their own.

The following examples show different ways of making simple finger and hand puppets.

Five-Finger Rhyme
Dance, thumbkin, dance,
Dance, thumbkin, dance,
Dance ye merrymen every one,
But thumbkin he can dance alone,
Dance, thumbkin, dance.
(Repeat for foreman, middleman, ringman, and littleman.)

(Traditional)

Finger Puppets

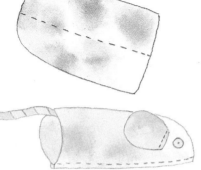

1 Make a small animal, using a scrap of felt or fur folded in half and stitched up the side. Stitch on a piece of string for the tail and bits of felt for the ears.

2 Cut the fingers from an old glove. Glue on eyes, nose, mouth, etc, using felt or paper scraps, feathers, buttons and beads.

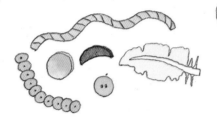

3 Draw a picture on firm cardboard, then cut it out. Make a ring of paper to fit the top of your finger and glue or tape it onto the back of the picture. You could cut out simple animal shapes or figures, then color them in and glue on scraps of material to decorate them.

4 Knit a puppet: Use medium weight yarn and size 3 needles.
Cast on 20 stitches.
Knit 26 rows.
Knit two together along the 27th row.
Cut the yarn, leaving a loose end of about 8 inches, and sew the end of the yarn back through

the stitches on the needle. Slide the stitches off the needle and pull the end of the yarn to gather them tightly together. Oversew the end to secure it. Sew the two edges together. Stuff the top with pieces of stocking or cotton to make a head, and gather the puppet tightly under the stuffing to make a neck. Make a face and some hair, using buttons and scraps of yarn.

5 Cut out a cardboard figure about 5 inches tall, without legs. Make two holes in the base of the trunk. Put your second and third fingers through the holes to give the puppet legs.

Hand Puppets

1 Use the palm of your hand. Simply draw on a face then wiggle your fingers and thumb and watch the face move.

2 Draw a face on a small paper bag. Tie up the two corners to represent ears. Or fold down the top of the bag to make a mouth that moves.

Five Little Ducks

Five little ducks went out to play,
Over the hills and far away.
Mother Duck said, "Quack, quack, quack,"
And only four little ducks came back.

(Repeat for four ducks, then three, then two, then one, then the final verse:)

Mother Duck went out one day,
Over the hills and far away.
Mother Duck said, "Quack, quack, quack,"
And five little ducks came swimming back.

(Traditional)

Hinged and shadow puppets

Hinged Puppets

Practice making hinged puppets by cutting out a variety of shapes from stiff cardboard and joining them together with paper fasteners so that the various parts can be moved.

Dragons

Cut a dragon's body out of stiff cardboard in three separate pieces—the head, the body, and the tail. Join the pieces together using paper fasteners so that the separate pieces each have a certain amount of movement. Tape one stick to the head part and one to the tail part.

Jumping Jack

Cut out one piece of cardboard in the shape of a body and head, then cut out two arms and two legs. Fasten the arms and legs to the body with paper fasteners so they can move freely.

Using three pieces of strong thread (one long piece and two short pieces):
a) make two small holes in the top of the arms and thread one short piece through the holes to join them together;
b) make two holes in the top of the legs and use the other short piece of thread to join these together;

c) tie the long piece of thread to the middle of the two short pieces leaving about 6 inches hanging below the body.

Make a hole in the top of the head and reinforce it with tape. Thread a piece of string through the hole. Hang the puppet up by this piece of string. Pull the hanging thread (c) to make the puppet jump.

Shadow Puppets

Cut out silhouettes of animals or figures from stiff cardboard and tape a stick to each one. To make groups of animals (for example, three mice) stick the silhouettes onto a strip of strong card to form a base, then tape a stick to the base. Choose characters from favorite rhymes or stories.

Make a translucent screen. For example, hang a white bedsheet across part of an open doorway or down the side of a table. Make sure the screen is as smooth and firmly held as possible. Use a table lamp or desk lamp to shine a light on the back of the screen and darken the rest of the room.

The puppet player stands on the same side as the light and holds up the puppets against the screen. The audience sits on the other side of the screen so that they see the puppets' shadows on the screen.

Making masks

Always make large eye holes in masks so your child can see clearly. The eye holes can be in addition to the eyes for the mask face if you want to decorate the eyes for the face.

1 Cut the back and the opened end off a cereal box and make a hole in each side of the box. Thread some elastic through the holes to hold the mask in place. Paint over the box or cover it with plain paper, then decorate it with scraps of material or paper. Cut out the eye holes, and a flap for the nose if you wish.

2 Decorate a paper bag; cut holes for the eyes and tie up the corners to make ears. If the bag is a long one, cut up the sides a little so that it will fit over your child's shoulders.

3 Decorate a paper plate and either thread elastic through it to hold it in place, or tape it onto a stick to make a handle to hold the mask in front of the face.

4 Use the shape shown in the illustration below as a guide, and cut out a similar shape from stiff cardboard. Make it large enough to fit around your child's head. Mark out the shape of the eyes lightly in pencil and then cut them out. Bend the straps a, b, and c into position and then adjust them to fit the head. Glue the straps into position. Make a paper cone for a nose, and glue on some ears, or a cone hat, and yarn or string hair.

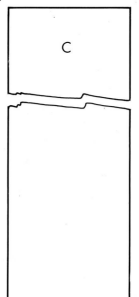

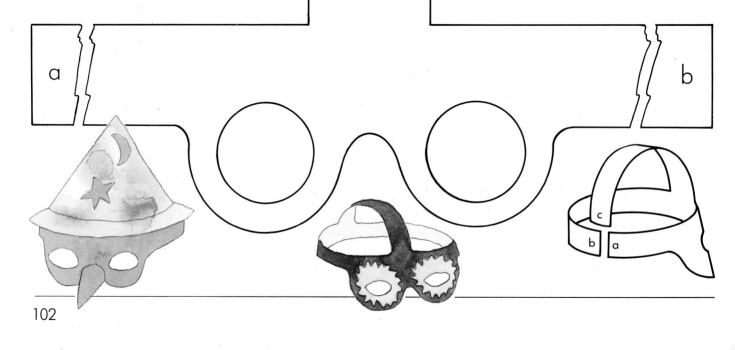

Dressing up

Collect a box of interesting and colorful old clothes and fabric. Particularly useful are things that can be used in several ways, such as skirts, shoes, scarves, shawls, shirts, hats, ties. Also objects that suggest particular characteristics or occupations, such as glasses (without lenses), hats, uniforms, bags, a tool box, and so on.

Dressing-Up Games

1 Pick-a-person: Scatter the clothes around the room. One person stands in the middle of the room and another person gives directions, for example, "Walk forward," "Turn to the door," "Take two steps," "Stop." At the word "Stop," the person being directed picks up the nearest item of clothing and puts it on. Repeat this until they have picked up about four pieces of clothing, then look in a mirror (a full-length mirror is best). Talk about who the person might be who would dress like that. Make up a name for the character or a few words that would describe the character.

2 Suitcase game: Put a pile of old clothes and props on the floor and put an empty cardboard box alongside them. One person picks up an article, for example, a red hat, and puts it in the box saying, "I'm going on vacation and I will take . . . . my red hat." The next person also puts something in the box, for example, a blue shirt, and says "I'm going on vacation and I'll take . . . my red hat and blue shirt."

Continue the game, increasing the list of things in the box until one person forgets something.

3 "And a-this-a-way": Think of some characters you all know well, such as those from nursery rhymes, favorite stories, or television characters. One person thinks of a character and dresses up to look like them. Then they move around in the way that the character would, saying:

"When I was a lady (gentleman/ king/little boy, or whatever) And a . . . . was I, A-this-a-way and a-this-a-way And a-this-a-way went I."

4 Clothing store: Sort the clothes into different "departments"—hats, shoes, coats, and so on. Buy and sell them, introducing words such as too small, larger, thick, thin, short, heavy, light, and dark.

Acting games

Lots of nursery rhymes and poems are fun to act out. Here are a few ideas, but you and your child will probably have more favorites of your own.

Going to the Sea
Walk:
Walking in my red shoes,
Down the busy street,
Walking in my red shoes,
Whom do you think we'll
    meet?
"Hello, Jane."
Tramp:
Tramping in my black
    shoes,
Down the muddy lane,
Tramping in my black
    shoes
Through the dripping rain.
Skip:
Skipping on my bare toes,
Beside the sandy sea,
Up the beach and back again,
Up the beach and back again
And into the rolling sea.
Swim:
I swim – and I swim,
On the billows – I ride,
I float – and I float
With the swing of the
    tide.
Skip:
Then out of the sea,
And on to the sand,
I skippety-skip
To the beat of the band
And away from the rolling
    sea.
                (Ruth Sansom)

Elephant Walk
Plonk on this foot,
Plonk on that,
Swinging my trunk,
Swinging my trunk.
I'm out in the jungle
Without any hat,
Plonk on this,
Plonk on that!
I'll go to sleep
In the shade of a tree,
Nose on knee,
Nose on knee,
And no one will know
That it's only me,
Nod and nod,
Sleep and sleep.
                (Ruth Sansom)

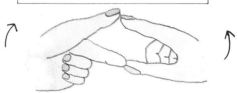

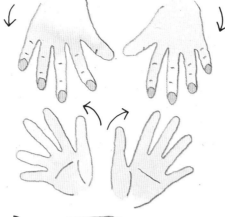

Eentsy Weentsy Spider
(Use hand movements only for this, as shown in the diagrams opposite.)
Verse 1:
Eentsy Weentsy Spider
Climbed up the water spout,
Verse 2:
Down came the rain
And washed the spider
    out.
Verse 3:
Out came the sun and
Dried up all the rain
Verse 4:
And Eentsy Weentsy Spider
Climbed up the spout
    again.
                (Traditional)

Simon Says

One person leads, saying, "Simon says do this" and at the same time making a simple movement. The other person imitates the action. As your child improves at the game, make it a little harder by occasionally omitting the words "Simon says" and just saying, "Do this." When this happens the other player must not copy the action. If they do, they will be "out" and they become the leader.

Shadows

Hang up an old sheet, or clear a space on a white wall, to act as a "screen." Shine a light onto your screen and put your hands, or your whole body, in front of the light to cast a shadow. See how many shadow shapes you can make. For example, you can use your hands to make a bird or a rabbit's head with floppy ears, and use your body to make a gorilla or a monster.

Telephones

Make your own telephone by joining two yogurt containers with a piece of string. Poke a hole in the bottom of each container. Then thread one end of the string through each container and knot it. Pull the containers apart so that the string is taut. One person speaks into one container, while the other person listens through the "receiver."

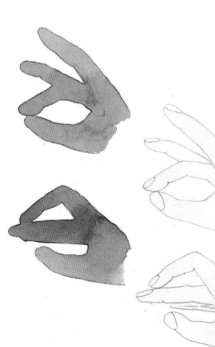

Hands
Hands are very handy things,
Hands can wash things,
Hands can squash things,
Hands can gently pat your head.
Hands can clap,
Hands can flap,
Hands can point like this or that.
Hands can make things,
Hands can shake things,
Hands can flutter, just like wings.
Hands can fold,
Hands can hold,
Hands are very handy things.

(Ogden Nash)

Using words

Shopping Lists

Build up a list of words (this trains the memory, too). One person begins by saying, "I went to the store and bought . . .," then naming one item. The next person repeats the sentence including the item and adds a purchase of their own. The game continues until someone forgets the list.

To play the game with younger children—put a variety of objects out on the table. As they are named, the objects are picked up and moved to the front of the table.

The same game can be played with a different introductory line, for example, "In the zoo there were . . . . elephants" and so on.

Feelies

Hide some toys or other objects in paper bags. Ask your child to put a hand into each bag in turn and guess what is inside without looking. Ask them to describe each object as they feel it, for example, "It is hard . . . cold . . . rough . . . smooth . . . round . . . hollow . . . solid . . . curved . . . crooked". . . and so on.

Similes

How many words can you think of to fill these gaps?

As quiet as . . . . . .
As loud as . . . . . .
As hard as . . . . . .
As small as . . . . . .

Change the sentences to be appropriate to whatever you are doing at the time

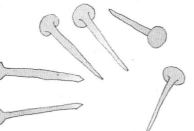

Riddles

Invent some "What am I" riddles.
For example:

1. Riddle me! riddle me!
   What is that
   Over your head and under
      your hat?
(Answer: hair)

2. With my little eye,
   Nothing can I spy,
   But, BEWARE
   A sharp point have I.
(Answer: needle)

3. It scratches and tugs
   And hurt it might,
   But its sharp teeth
   Can never bite.
(Answer: comb)

Tongue Twisters

There are many good tongue twisters. See if you can invent some of your own. Here are a few just to start you off:

1. Moses supposes his toeses
      are roses,
   But Moses supposes
      erroneously;
   For nobody's toeses are
      posies of roses
   As Moses supposes his toeses
      to be.
2. Billy Button bought a buttered
      biscuit.
   Did Billy Button buy a
      buttered biscuit?
   If Billy Button bought a
      buttered biscuit,
   Where's the buttered biscuit
      that Billy Button bought?
3. She sells seashells on the
      seashore.

Playing with Words

As you sing or say familiar nursery rhymes, try putting in the wrong word for your listeners to spot the mistake. For example:
   Baa Baa Black *cow* (sheep)
   Have you any wool?
   Yes sir, yes sir,
   Three bags *sausages* (full)
   One for the master
   One for the *kangaroo* (dame)
   And one for the little boy
      who lives down the lane.
Or leave out the second of two rhyming words for someone else to fill in the gap:
   Little Polly Flinders,
   Sat among the . . . .
      (cinders)
   Warming her pretty little toes.
   Her mother came and caught
      her,
   And whipped her little
      . . . . (daughter)
   For spoiling her nice new
      clothes.

Illustrating Words

Draw some words on a large sheet of paper and decorate them to give a clue to their meaning.

Question and Answer Poems

Make up rhyming words to answer questions—the words can be nonsensical, as long as they rhyme. For example:

What's your name?
  Sarah Jane.
Where do you live?
  In a sieve.
What's your number?
  Cucumber.
What's your town?
  Upside down.

Moving to Words

Think of some words that are fun to say: hiss, hoop, tiptoe, pop, buzz, giggle, showery, drippy, zoo, slide, oblong, slipper, wobble, and so on.

Invent movements (flicking fingers, flapping, stabbing, winding, curling, stretching) to accompany some of the words—move around the room repeating them. Experiment with the way you say the words (whispering, shouting, singing). Try using instruments that match the sounds of the words as you say them (see pages 95–97).

Sound Words

Make up words to match familiar sounds and noises, like the sound of a vacuum cleaner, or rain falling, or people walking in boots or soft slippers.

Rat-a-Tat Tat

Rat-a-tat tat
Who is that?
Only grandma's pussycat.
What do you want?
A pint of milk.
Where is your money?
In my pocket.
Where is your pocket?
I forgot it.
Oh you silly pussycat!

(Traditional)

In the Rain

Swishing, swashing down the lane,
Come the trucks in the rain.
Shunkle, shonkle is the mutter,
Of water flowing down the gutter.
Shillop, shallop through the mud,
Go the cows chewing the cud.
Splashing, splishing, cars go by,
But I'm inside and nice and dry!

(Daphne Lister)

Action poems

Try saying the following poems and make the actions to go with them. In the first poem, the first two verses represent a train approaching the crest of a hill. In the last verse the train races down the hill.

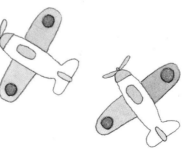

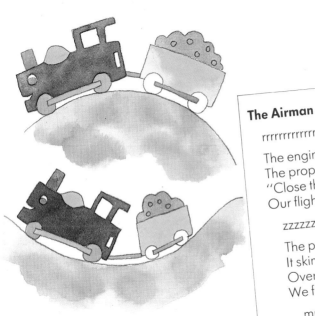

The Airman

rrrrrrrrrrrr

The engine roars,
The propeller spins,
"Close the doors!"
Our flight begins.

zzzzzzzzzzzzz

The plane rises;
It skims the trees.
Over the houses
We fly at our ease.

mmmmmm

ZOOM goes the plane,
The engine hums.
Then home again,
And down it comes . . . . .

(Clive Sansom)

Eletelephony

Once there was an elephant
Who tried to use the telephant—
No! No! I mean an elephone
Who tried to use the telephone—
(Dear me! I am not certain quite
That even now I've got it right.)

Howe're it was, he got his trunk
Entangled in the telephunk,
The more he tried to get it free,
The louder buzzed the telephee—
(I fear I'd better drop the song
of elephop and telephong!)

(Laura E. Richards)

The Steam Train and the Hill

I wish I could
   I wish I could
      I wish I could

I think I can
   I think I can
      I think I can.

I thought I could,
   I thought I could,
      I thought I could . . . . .

(Clive Sansom)

Story ideas

(For telling, not reading)

1 For first stories, look for simple ideas:
A walk in the park
A visit to a store
A day at the beach

2 Make up stories about the people you see on the street outside your house, such as the delivery man, mailman, newsboy or girl. Take each person in turn and describe what happens as they visit three or four houses. Is anyone at home? Is a note left? How many packages or letters are delivered? Does the newsboy or girl whistle loudly?

Children enjoy stories with repetition as they can guess what's going to happen, so introduce repetition into your stories—at the fourth house a dog always barks and scares the visitor away, so they are left with no letters or papers.

3 The train journey: Draw a railroad track across a blackboard or sheet of paper. Then move a cardboard or toy train along the track, describing what the passengers see. As you talk, paste on pictures or draw simple stick people and animals to illustrate the story.

A walk around the town (farm, zoo, park, or whatever) can be told in the same way.

4 "It has to be something special:" Draw a plan of the stores in a shopping mall. Sarah is moving from store to store, looking for a birthday present for her mother, and food for a birthday party. Invent a conversation that can be repeated in every store (perhaps using the words in the title); eventually she finds the right present.

5 "Where do I live?": Draw a simple picture to illustrate the story given below. Give your child a duck made of cardboard or plastic to move across the picture as the duck in the story waddles around the farm.

The Story

A duckling leaves his nest and goes for a walk.

Tired and lonely, he realizes he has forgotten where he lives. He sees a hole in the ground, looks in and asks "Is this where I live?"

"No!" Out jumps a fox and says, "This is my home." And the fox frightens the duckling away.

Repeat the same formula with the duck looking into a tree at a bird's nest, finding a mouse's nest among the wheat, a chicken's nest in the barn, finally, a boy in the farmhouse. The boy then picks up the duckling and takes him to the pond where his mother is waiting.

As an alternative: draw the picture on a blackboard, putting in each piece as you tell the story.

Scrapbooks

Cut some sheets of thick plain or colored paper to about 10 inches by 16 inches and fold them in half. Either staple along the fold to hold the sheets together (although this can make them hard to open out) or sew down the fold. Keep your first scrapbooks short (about four pages only). Write your child's name in clear letters on the front so that he or she feels the importance of having their own book.

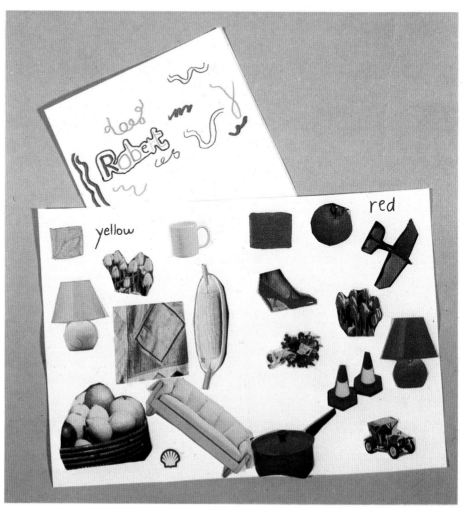

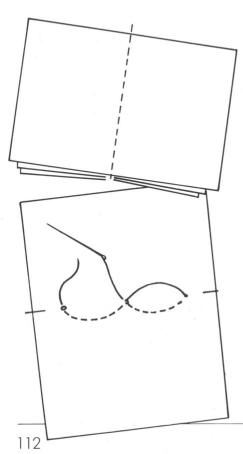

Topics

1 A collection of pictures (cut from magazines)—encourage your child to group them according to their subject. For example, a page for food, clothes, flowers, and so on.

2 Colors—if your child has just learned to distinguish colors, why not make a book with one page for each color? Put a dab of the particular color at the top of the page and write the name of the color alongside; underneath, glue pictures from magazines and your child's own drawings in the same color.

3 Me—include some photographs and/or your child's own drawings of their family, house, toys, and pets. Write the names of each in a simple sentence underneath.

Shaping letters

When writing for your children, on their paintings or books, be particularly careful about forming your letters clearly. Always use letters in lower case (i.e. "small" letters), except when a capital letter is necessary, such as for the first letter of a proper name—Mark, Lisa.

The letters shown on this page are one example of a style to follow. I have also included arrows to show how the letters are formed. For more information on teaching children to write see pages 114–120.

Getting ready to read and write

The best way to prepare children for reading is by showing them a good example. Share your enjoyment of books with them and read to them regularly. Visit the children's section of your local library. If you have any adult reference books with colorful and interesting illustrations in them, show these to your child as well.

I have not attempted to describe the teaching of reading and writing in detail here, as this has already been thoroughly covered in other books. However, in this chapter you will find some additional ideas for games to help your child develop these vital skills.

Pencil Control
Remember that pencil control does not come easily to most children so never try to force it. Use large crayons to begin with and let your child cover the paper with dots, dashes, a continuous winding line, or crosses.

1 Draw any of the patterns shown here for your child to trace over with a crayon. Or use any simple patterns you can think of.

2 Start off the patterns shown below, for your child to continue.

3 Make the patterns more fun by combining several together, or turn some of them into pictures after your child has traced the basic pattern.

4 Draw five pictures on one side of a piece of paper. On the opposite side, in a different order, draw five other pictures that are related to the first ones. Then ask your child to join them up into pairs with a pencil line.

Following the same idea, join words to pictures; or for older children, join identical words or words in rhyming pairs.

5 Draw some simple mazes which move across the page either from left to right, or from top to bottom. Or draw "tangles" to be sorted out, such as three balloons with three tangled strings. Let your child find the right routes by drawing over them with a crayon.

Observing details

Place a few objects on the table and ask your child to look at them carefully, taking note of their relative positions. Then ask your child to close her eyes while you remove an object. Can she guess which object is missing? As your child gains experience, more items can be added to make the game more difficult.

Working From Left to Right
Make the following games with strips of cardboard about 2 inches by 8 inches.

1 Find the pair: Draw a simple object on the left-hand side of the card and separate it off from the rest of the card with a colored line. Then draw three or four other objects on the card—one of which is identical to the first object.

Encourage your child to work from left to right as he picks out the identical object.

2 Make up some cards as before, but this time use stick people performing different actions. Again, match one of the actions to the drawing on the far left of the card. Your child could imitate the actions of the stick people, too.

3 To make the game a bit harder, try drawing faces with different expressions; for example, smiling with eyes open, smiling with eyes shut, sad with eyes open, sad with eyes shut, tears in eyes and no tears.

4 Spot the difference: Make some other sets of cards showing rows of objects, all but one of which are identical. Then try doing this with letters too.

Learning letters

1 Write letters using as many different tools as you can, such as steamed-up windows, a tray of sand, or using a thick paintbrush on newspaper.

2 Try to make the shapes of letters with your hands—perhaps by using shadows on a sunny wall.

3 Look for letters on food packaging, newspapers, and magazines. Make up cards for each letter showing all the different ways they can appear in print.

4 Make up some other cards with two or three versions of two or three letters all mixed up. Ask your child to find the versions of one letter.

Or, cut out some words which each contain one particular letter (such as "a"). Then ask your child to find and circle that letter in each word.

5 Cut out letters from black paper and trace them onto a sheet of white paper. Let your child match the silhouette to the outline.

6 Play "Find the pair" and "Spot the difference" as described on the previous pages, but this time use letters instead of objects.

Letter games

1 Make a set of twelve pairs of letter cards to play some simple card games like snap and pairs.

2 Make a simple board game with some squares colored in—as shown in the illustration. Put a stack of letter cards face down in the middle of the board. Take turns to throw a die and move around the board. When a player lands on a colored square he or she has to pick up a letter card and say the name of the letter. If the answer is right the player wins another throw of the die.

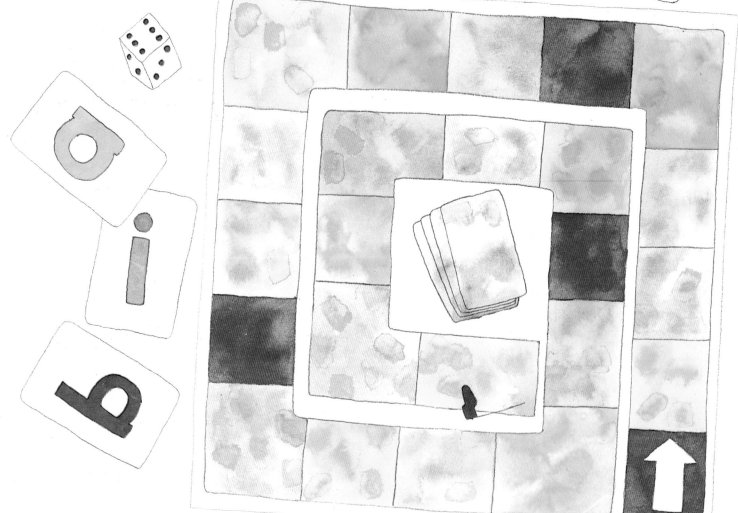

Learning words

Making and Using Word Cards

As you read simple books with your child, print the words they are learning in large letters onto pieces of cardboard. Always be certain that the words you use have first been read within the context of a sentence.

1 Let your child search for simple words ("and," "the," "my") in his or her books, then match the word to the appropriate word card.

2 Make cards showing the names of members of your family. Use them as place-names on chairs or at the table.

3 Label objects in the house. Extend this idea to introducing short phrases as well, such as "John's chair" and "Mary's cup."

4 Posters made out of pictures cut from magazines can also be labeled.

Action Cards

Once your child is beginning to feel confident with reading words, there are many ways to encourage their understanding of words. Here are a few suggestions:

1 Draw stick people on cards with each one performing a different action. Write the word for the action on the appropriate card. Hold up the cards one at a time for your child to read the word and imitate the action.

2 Write out simple instruction cards for different actions. Place the cards in a line across the room. Your child has to move from one card to the next, reading and then carrying out the instructions.

3 Hide an object and give your child a card which tells them where to find it. For example, "look under the table." As their skill improves, extend the hunt by hiding the cards around the house, one card giving the clue to the next and the final one leading to the "treasure."

Word games

Sorting
There are many ways to sort words. For example, word cards can be mailed into boxes according to their initial letters, or into trays according to their subject matter.

Card Games
Use the word cards, either by themselves or with matching picture cards, to play snap, pairs, lotto, and dominoes.

Adjectives
Cut out pictures from magazines and birthday cards (or draw them) to illustrate adjectives. Paste them on cards and write the adjective and noun underneath, for example, "thin dog," "fat dog," and so on.

Hidden Pictures
Fold a card firmly in half. Write a word that your child has learned on the outside and glue a picture to illustrate the word on the inside. If your child has difficulty reading the word, he or she can use the picture as a clue.

Plurals
Take a card and fold a third of it back. Write down the singular of any noun that forms its plural with an "s" (dog, cat, ball, bird, hat) on the front of the card on the left-hand side. Write the "s" on the far side of the folded piece so that when it is folded on top of the card the word becomes a plural. Illustrate the word and the "s" with matching pictures.

Fishing
Slip a paper clip onto each of your word cards and put them into a large cardboard box. Make a fishing rod using a stick, and some string with a magnet tied to the end of it. Take turns fishing out a card and read it out loud. Any that can't be read are thrown back into the "pond" for another turn (but be sure to read aloud the word first so that the next time it is caught it may be remembered).

Opposites
Make some more cards that will illustrate opposites, such as "up" and "down," "in" and "out," "on" and "off."